PENGUIN PLAYS

BAR MITZVAH BOY
AND OTHER TELEVISION PLAYS

In 1975, *The Evacuees* won the International Emmy Award, the British Academy of Film and Television Arts Best Play Award and the Broadcasting Press Guild Best Play Award.

In 1976, *Bar Mitzvah Boy* won the British Academy Best Play Award and the Broadcasting Press Guild Best Play Award.

In 1977, *Spend, Spend, Spend* won the British Academy Best Play Award and nomination for the Italia Prize.

Jack Rosenthal was born in Manchester in 1931. He read English at Sheffield University and Russian (badly) in the Royal Navy. He began writing for television in 1961 with Episode 30 of *Coronation Street* and went on to write a further 150 episodes, as well as scores of scripts for many drama and comedy series, including *That Was The Week That Was*. He originated three comedy series of his own: *The Dustbinmen*, *The Lovers* (Writers' Guild Best Comedy Series Award, 1971) and *Sadie, It's Cold Outside*.

Apart from the three which comprise this anthology, Jack Rosenthal has written some twenty-two plays including *Another Sunday and Sweet F.A.* (TV Critics' Circle Award, 1972), *Ready When You Are, Mr McGill* (British Academy Best nomination, 1976), *Auntie's Niece*, *Your Name's Not God – It's Edgar*, *Polly Put the Kettle On*, *Mr Ellis Versus the People*, *There'll Almost Always Be an England*, *Well, Thank You, Thursday*, *The Knowledge*, *P'tang Yang Kipperbang*, *Mrs Capper's Birthday*, *The Fools on the Hill*, *London's Burning*, *Day to Remember*, *Sleeping Sickness* and *Bag Lady*. His feature films include *Lucky Star*, *Yentl* (co-written with Barbra Streisand) and *The Chain*.

In 1976, he won the British Academy Writer's Award and the Royal Television Society Writer's Award.

He lives in London with his wife, actress Maureen Lipman, their daughter, Amy, and son, Adam.

JACK ROSENTHAL

BAR MITZVAH BOY
and Other Television Plays

Bar Mitzvah Boy
The Evacuees
Spend, Spend, Spend

Penguin Books

PENGUIN BOOKS

Published by the Penguin Group
Penguin Books Ltd, 27 Wrights Lane, London W8 5TZ, England
Penguin Books USA Inc., 375 Hudson Street, New York, New York 10014, USA
Penguin Books Australia Ltd, Ringwood, Victoria, Australia
Penguin Books Canada Ltd, 10 Alcorn Avenue, Toronto, Ontario, Canada M4V 3B2
Penguin Books (NZ) Ltd, 182–190 Wairau Road, Auckland 10, New Zealand

Penguin Books Ltd, Registered Offices: Harmondsworth, Middlesex, England

First published in Penguin Books as *Three Award-winning Television Plays* 1978
Reprinted as *Bar Mitzvah Boy and Other Television Plays* 1987
3 5 7 9 10 8 6 4

Printed in England by Clays Ltd, St Ives plc
Set in Monotype Baskerville

Contents

Note

The following abbreviations of technical terms
are used throughout the three plays:

Ext.	Exterior
Int.	Interior
C.U.	Close up
O.O.V.	Out of vision
P.O.V.	Point of view
V.O.	Voice over

Bar Mitzvah Boy

First transmission date 14 September 1976

Produced by Graeme McDonald
Directed by Michael Tuchner

ELIOT GREEN	Jeremy Steyn
DENISE	Kim Clifford
SQUIDGE	Mark Herman
LESLEY GREEN	Adrienne Posta
RITA GREEN	Maria Charles
SYLVIA	Pamela Manson
SALON CUSTOMER	Sabina Michael
SOLLY	Harry Landis
VICTOR GREEN	Bernard Spear
HAROLD	Jonathan Lynn
GRANDAD	Cyril Shaps
RABBI SHERMAN	Jack Lynn
CARETAKER	Robert Putt
WARDEN	Harold Reese

1. Ext. Street in Willesden. Mid-afternoon.

[*Two or three groups of schoolchildren are slouching (or racing, or cavorting) their way home from school. Most of them are in school uniform, albeit well-worn and dishevelled, and they carry satchels. The last group consists of* ELIOT, *aged thirteen; his pal,* SQUIDGE, *a little older; and* DENISE, *also about thirteen.*
DENISE, *in the middle of a heated harangue, rounds on* ELIOT.]

DENISE: Oh, you lying bugger, you *did*!
SQUIDGE: Ignore her.
ELIOT: I am.
SQUIDGE: Maintain an aloof silence.
DENISE: He did, though, Squidge! *Somebody* did.
ELIOT [*to* DENISE]: For your information, I don't split on people in Geography. I didn't know you had *any* book under the desk. Let alone that one.
DENISE [*not at all convinced*]: Well, somebody did . . .
   [ELIOT *slows down on reaching his house.*]
ELIOT: See you then, Squidge.
SQUIDGE: Are we going swimming tomorrow?
ELIOT [*incredulously*]: You must be quipping!
SQUIDGE: Why must I?
ELIOT: Tomorrow???
SQUIDGE [*puzzled by his reaction*]: Bloody tomorrow!
ELIOT: You know what tomorrow is, don't you?
SQUIDGE: Saturday.
ELIOT: Only the day that marks my passage, isn't it!
DENISE: The what?
SQUIDGE [*apprehensive on* ELIOT's *behalf*]: Oh, hell, I forgot!
ELIOT: You're lucky!
DENISE [*to* SQUIDGE]: What is it? What passage?
SQUIDGE [*to* ELIOT]: And are you scared rigid? I was scared rigid at *mine*. I made sixteen mistakes in the Hebrew bit. Sixteen at least. Probably twenty-five or

9

something. And I forgot half my speech at the reception. Three quarters nearly. I missed out mentioning my Uncle Gus and Auntie Merle. And cousins from America. I missed out everybody. I was deadly.

ELIOT: I'll see you Sunday, though.

SQUIDGE: If you survive, mate. Mon ami. Meus amicus.

ELIOT: I'll survive.

[ELIOT *continues on his way to the back door of his house.* SQUIDGE *and* DENISE *walk on,* SQUIDGE *with his arm round* DENISE'S *shoulder*].

DENISE [*puzzled*]: What's he mean? 'Marks his passage'? Is it rude?

SQUIDGE: It's something Jewish. What Jewish boys do. You wouldn't understand.

DENISE [*suspicious*]: It *sounds* rude.

[*They walk on.*]

2. Int. Kitchen. (Continuous in time.)

[*A key turns in the lock, the door opens and* ELIOT *walks in. Reflexively, from habit, he kisses his finger then places the finger on the Mezuzah on the doorpost – all very briefly while walking in.* ELIOT'S *usual demeanour of solemnity, earnestness and pre-occupation – from which he was diverted during his row with* DENISE *– now returns. To stay.*]

ELIOT [*calling*]: It's only me. [*He closes the door, slings his satchel down, and starts peeling off his raincoat.*] [*Calling*] C'est seulement moi. [*He opens the fridge, takes a piece of gefilte fish from it. Takes a bite.*] [*Calling*] Est solus ego. [*He drops his coat on to the floor, takes a piece of cake from a cake tin, starts peeling off his school blazer and exits to living room.*]

3. Int. Living room.

[ELIOT *enters from the kitchen, munching fish and cake in turn.*]

ELIOT [*calling*]: Anyone at home? [*He drops his blazer on to the floor, and takes an orange from a fruitbowl on the sideboard.*] [*Calling*] Est-il quelqu'un dans la maison? [*He starts towards the hall.*] [*Calling*] Est quisquam – or whatever it is – in domo? [*He exits into the hall.*]

4. Int. Hall and stairs.

[ELIOT *enters from the living room. He slings his cap at the hall-stand. It misses and falls to the floor. He starts up the stairs.*

ELIOT [*shouting with bravado, now knowing there's no one to hear him*]: Naked women! Les femmes nues! Nudae feminae!
  [*He disappears from view up the stairs.*
  A key turns in the lock, the front door opens and LESLEY *enters with extreme difficulty – laden and overladen with parcels of shopping. As she enters, the phone in the living room starts ringing.*]
LESLEY [*calling*]: Eliot? Answer the . . . I've got my hands . . . Eliot! Are you in?
ELIOT [*O.O.V. upstairs*]: No.
LESLEY: Don't answer the phone, will you!
ELIOT [*O.O.V.*]: No.
LESLEY: I mean – don't help! I'm only up to my . . . I've got ten thousand . . .
  [*The phone continues to ring.*
  LESLEY *– irritated, frustrated – drops her parcels on to the floor, picks up* ELIOT'S *cap out of habit and races with it to the living room.*]

5. Int. Living room.

[LESLEY *dashes in and picks up the phone.*]
LESLEY [*into phone*]: Billy Smart's Circus, Lesley Green speaking. [*Pause.*] Hello, Mum. [*Pause.*] What circus? I didn't mention circus. [*Pause.*] Well, of *course* I knew it was you. [*Pause.*] In this family, it *pays* to be psychic. It was ringing when I walked in. *Ran* in. I've been running all afternoon. My legs just do it – I don't ask them. Where are you?

6. Int. Sylvia's hairdressing salon.

[*A fifth-rate tiny, local shop in the front room of* SYLVIA'S *house. The sort that bear a sign in the front window offering, in plastic letters, 'De luxe styling'.*

SYLVIA, *the proprietress, silently and habitually frantic, is attending to two or three of her customers' hair (all in different stages of preparation) virtually at the same time. One of them, her hair in the middle of being shampooed, is* RITA. *She's speaking into the phone from a hairdresser's chair, the cradle of the phone in her lap.*]

RITA: Well, where?
LESLEY [*O.O.V.*]: Where?
RITA: That's an interesting question.
LESLEY [*O.O.V.*]: Is there any chance of an answer?
RITA: Still at Sylvia's . . . where else would I be? The day everything runs smooth, I'll get a telegram from the Queen. [*Pause.*] *No* one's fault. Sylvia couldn't start on me till after three.
SYLVIA: I'm not a magician.
RITA: She's not a magician. Mrs Mickler was before me, and she was late, what could I do? With her abdomen and suspected conjunctivitis, I'm going to fall out with the woman? Listen, did you get the dry-cleaning?

[*Intercut as required between* RITA *in the salon and* LESLEY *in the living room.*]

LESLEY: They're all lunatics in there. They should have a sign up – Lunatic Dry-Cleaners Limited.

RITA: Did you get the cleaning?

LESLEY: First, they say Dad's suit won't be ready till Monday . . .

RITA: Oh, my God!

SYLVIA: Bad news? I hope I'm wrong.

LESLEY: Then they can't find it . . .

RITA: He needs it tomorrow!

LESLEY: Then it must be at another branch . . .

RITA: So you haven't got it!

LESLEY: I've got it. I've got it. It was there all the time. They're lunatics.

RITA: Listen, Lesley. I'm going to be a couple of hours yet.

SYLVIA: At least.

RITA: At least. Now the brisket's in the oven . . . Put it on a low light to warm up, do a few potatoes with it, and open a tin of peas . . . I'll be home before it's ready.

SYLVIA: Please God.

RITA: Please God. And, Lesley. Listen. Tell Eliot to go and have his hair cut. His dad's there now having his, so he'll see him there. And Lesley. *Make* him. Any arguing, tell him no arguing. Threaten. And, listen. Lesley. Hang up the dry-cleaning in the wardrobe . . . not in the wardrobe, *outside* the wardrobe because of the chemicals, and if you've a minute . . .

LESLEY: Mother, where do I get a minute? Where from? I'd *enjoy* having one! All day I've been running.

RITA: If you've a minute, ring the caterers.

LESLEY: What for?

RITA: Just 'Hello, is that the caterers, I'm speaking on behalf of Mrs Green, is everything all right for tomorrow?' I'll be happier.

LESLEY: Mother, please stop panicking. You want me to have cold sores at the dinner-dance?

RITA: What cold sores?

LESLEY: You give me cold sores. Every time I put an evening dress on I have a cold sore to match. The *J.C.* prints it under Forthcoming Attractions ... 'The Green Family must be having a simcha, Lesley's got a lipful of cold sores.'

[*She puts the phone down.*
Cut to salon. RITA *replaces the receiver.*]

RITA [*addressing no one in particular*]: Cold sores she's drikking me with ...

FIRST CUSTOMER [*as* SYLVIA *flits about her hair*]: You're having caterers?

RITA: Levy's. A hundred and seventeen guests at £7.50 a head. Or £7.50 a tochass, depending which way you look at it. If you're wondering where the money's coming from – so am I. And that's without lemon sorbet.

SECOND CUSTOMER: A wedding, is it?

RITA: Bar mitzvah. My son, Eliot. He gets bar mitzvah'd tomorrow.

FIRST CUSTOMER: Mazeltov.

RITA: Thank you – I'm having tips and streaks.

SYLVIA [*scanning the room in restrained frenzy*]: Things get up and walk in this place. I had scissors.

SECOND CUSTOMER [*passing them to her*]: Scissors.

SYLVIA [*taking them and starting on her hair*]: Who can get staff these days? You try and run a business ... The younger generation don't *want* to work. I don't blame them. I *also* would rather be a pop star. I'm waiting for someone to *ask*.

7. Int. Eliot's Bedroom.

[ELIOT *is lying on his bed, munching desultorily from the small store of food he harvested en route from the kitchen. He's looking solemnly round the room at the acquisitions of his childhood ...*

wallposters of pop stars and sports stars, shelves of model aircraft, books and toys.
Suddenly he gets up and starts rapidly taking his posters from the wall, rolling them up and dropping them into a waste-paper basket. One by one, the models, books and toys are slung into the basket.]

8. Int. Hallway.

[LESLEY *is gathering up her dropped parcels. She stops half-way through to put* ELIOT'S *cap and her own coat on to the hallstand. Then continues gathering up her parcels.*
ELIOT *strolls downstairs. He holds a prayerbook in his hand.*]

LESLEY: I thought you said you were out.
ELIOT: Objection overruled. I said I wasn't in.
LESLEY: Isn't that the same thing?
ELIOT: Squidge says nothing's the same as anything else. Except nothing.
LESLEY: Yes, he would.
    [*She half-runs, with her parcels, to the living room.* ELIOT *trails behind her.*]

9. Int. Living room.

[LESLEY *enters, drops the parcels on the table and starts half-running to the kitchen.*]

LESLEY: Mum rang. You've to go for a haircut right away. No arguments. It's not being thrown open for debate. You just go.
    [ELIOT *enters from the hall, and follows her towards the kitchen, taking a banana from the fruitbowl en route.*]
ELIOT: Would you like to test me?

10. Int. Kitchen.

[LESLEY *enters, turning to* ELIOT *in mild horror on hearing his question.*]

LESLEY: Would you care to rephrase the question?

ELIOT [*entering*]: Please will you please test me please?

LESLEY: Like I've nothing else to do . . . like I'm having such a good time . . .

[*Still half-running, she starts the preparations for dinner, peeling potatoes etc.*

ELIOT *sits, in what appears to be the most uncomfortable position possible, at the small kitchen table. He watches her solemnly while eating his banana.*]

ELIOT: Not in Hebrew. Just the English.

LESLEY: Eliot! *Haircut! Now!*

ELIOT: Go on. [*He hands her the book.*] Please. S'il vous plaît. Si placet.

LESLEY: And stop that. It gets on my nerves.

ELIOT: Stop what? Arrêtez quoi? Prohibi quid?

LESLEY: It's not being clever, you know. It's just showing your ignorance. Nine times out of ten you get it wrong.

[*She continues working.*

ELIOT *opens his prayer-book at the relevant page and starts testing himself – glancing at the words, half-closing the book, closing his eyes, muttering to himself: then opening both book and eyes again at the next section on the page.*]

Eliot! Dad's *expecting* you there! He'll be worried!

11. Int. 'Solly the Barber's'.

[*A small, long-established family business, dishevelled, untidy, which has been specialising in 'short back and sides' ever since the thirties.*

Open on ELIOT'S *dad,* VICTOR. *He's not worried at all. He's laughing, hugely, dirtily (wheezing 'very good!' 'cracker!') at a joke that's just been told. He starts to take his chair before the mirror.*

Another two or three men are either waiting their turn on the bench or in other barber's chairs half-attended to.

SOLLY: Short back and sides?

VICTOR [*to* FIRST MAN]: Short back and sides, he asks me. Like I'm going to say no. Like I've been coming here for thirty years having a bloody bubble-cut or something. [*He pinches and wiggles* SOLLY'*s jowl affectionately.*] Chuchilla!

SOLLY: Short back and sides then.

VICTOR: Why not? Let's go mad.

   [SOLLY *starts preparing to cut* VICTOR'*s hair.*)

SOLLY: Here you are. Got another one for you. There's this Yiddishe feller walking down the street, and he sees this—

VICTOR [*to* FIRST MAN]: Always has to be a Yiddishe feller, have you noticed? Can't be a bloody Peruvian ...

SOLLY: ... And he sees this young dolly-bird in this whatisit ... miniskirt and he thinks 'Aye, aye. I wouldn't mind having a—'

VICTOR [*interrupting*]: Hey, a bloody punter gets in my cab this morning. A Yank. Sunglasses, camera, pink jacket, the whole gericht, wants to go to Richmond. So we've been going a couple of minutes, no trouble, and he says 'It won't take more than quarter of an hour, will it?' To Richmond! Like I'm in Leicester Square, aren't I! So I said 'This is a cab, darling. If you want a magic bloody carpet, I'll drop you off at Persian Airlines.' So he says 'Kush mir in tochass.' 'Kiss mine,' I says. So he looks at me and says 'Well, what do you know! Are you an American too?' Bloody nutter. I charged him 30p over the odds.

SOLLY: I'm telling you a good joke! I've got a good joke here! [*Resumes.*] So this Yiddishe feller's walking down the street, clocks the dolly-bird and thinks 'Aye, aye, I wouldn't mind having a—'

VICTOR: Have you seen *Shampoo*, Solly?

SOLLY: What shampoo?

VICTOR: The picture. *Shampoo*. All about a ladies' hairdresser. Warren Beatty. All he does is yentz. Every bird he sees, he yentzes. The whole picture's one long yentz. Well, not *one*. Bloody *hundreds*.

SOLLY: That's *Ladies'* Hairdressers. Me, I keep my hazen on and tell jokes.

12. Int. Kitchen.

[ELIOT *and* LESLEY *as before.*]

LESLEY: What I wouldn't give for a cup of tea.
    [ELIOT *leaps up to start making one.*]
Good God!

ELIOT [*filling the kettle*]: I like your dress, Lesley. I find it quite picturesque.
    [*She looks at him, amused despite herself.*]

LESLEY: Good God!

ELIOT [*offering the prayer-book to her.*]: Go on, Lesley! Just once. I do it tomorrow. You'll never have to test me again after this. Never in your whole life.
    [*She looks at him, feeling sudden sympathy.*
    A pause.]

LESLEY: You're not worried, are you, Eliot?

ELIOT: I meant it about your dress.
    [*She dries her hands and takes the book, already opened at the relevant page.*]

LESLEY: On your marks, get set, go.

ELIOT: 'And God spake these words, saying: I am the Lord thy God, who brought thee out of the land of Egypt, out of the house of bondage.'

13. Int. Sylvia's hairdressing salon.

[*Stay on* RITA'S *reflection as she sits before the mirror. Her hair is now a forest of tinfoil spikes.* SYLVIA *is adding the last couple.*]

ELIOT [*V.O.*] 'Thou shalt have no other gods before me. Thou shalt not make unto thee a graven image; nor the form of anything that is in heaven above, or that is in the earth beneath, or that is in the water under the earth; thou shalt not bow down thyself unto them, nor serve them.'

14. Int. 'Solly the Barber's'.

[*Stay on* VICTOR'S *reflection in the mirror, as* SOLLY *snips away at his hair.*]

ELIOT [*V.O.*] 'For I the Lord thy God am a jealous God, visiting the iniquity of the fathers upon the children, upon the third and upon the fourth generation, unto them that hate me: and showing lovingkindness to the thousandth generation, unto them that love me and keep my commandments.'

15. Int. Kitchen.

[ELIOT *is making* LESLEY'S *cup of tea.*
LESLEY *is still very busily preparing the evening meal, glancing irritatedly from time to time at the open prayer book beside her.*]

ELIOT: 'Thou shalt not take the name of the Lord thy God in vain,' etcetera.
LESLEY: 'Etcetera'????

ELIOT: 'Remember the Sabbath Day to keep it holy,' etcetera.

LESLEY [*peering incredulously at the page*]: There's a lot of 'etceteras' all of a sudden!

ELIOT: Well, you're busy. 'Honour thy father and thy mother, that thy days –'

LESLEY [*interrupting*]: Are you going for that haircut!! It's not a polite request. You like commandments? It was a commandment!

ELIOT [*very, very rapidly, almost without taking a breath*]: 'Thou shalt not murder. Thou shalt not commit adultery. Thou shalt not steal. Thou shalt not bear false witness. Thou shalt not covet thy neighbour's house, nor his wife, nor his man-servant nor his maidservant, nor his ox, nor his ass, nor his Allegro 1300, nor anything that is thy neighbour's.' The Allegro 1300's an optional extra. Joke.

[LESLEY *has been staring at him, incredulous at the speed of his delivery.*]

LESLEY: Well, I hope you're not just going to rattle it off like that! People'll be watching you!

ELIOT: People?

LESLEY: The family. The congregation. Rabbi Sherman. The choir.

ELIOT: Just people?

[LESLEY *looks at him, checked by – but not understanding – his question. He simply stares expressionlessly back at her. He then takes his prayer-book and another piece of gefilte fish from the fridge and exits to the living room.* LESLEY *watches him, troubled.*]

LESLEY [*calling brightly after him*]: Of course, *people*. People. Les personnages. Populus. What else *is* there? Giraffes?

[*There's no reply from* ELIOT.

LESLEY *stands disturbed, for a moment longer, then, busily resumes her work.*]

16. Int. Living room. Evening.

[*On the sideboard, the two Sabbath candles are burning.*
Seated around the table, the family are having dinner. RITA, *with her hair lacquered into stiff billows;* VICTOR, *with his short back and sides;* LESLEY; LESLEY'S *boyfriend,* HAROLD; *and* ELIOT.
Throughout the entire meal, ELIOT *picks at his meal with no appetite whatever. Occasionally, throughout the meal,* HAROLD *shoots affectionate (unreturned) smiles at* LESLEY. *Or takes her hand, surreptitiously for a second, before she withdraws it for the more important business of using knife, fork or spoon. Throughout the meal,* VICTOR *reads the evening paper.*
They eat their soup in silence for a few moments.]

RITA [*smiling with a frightening calm*]: It's horrible, isn't it?

LESLEY [*apprehensively*]: The soup?? I only warmed it up – you cooked it!

RITA: My hair.

[LESLEY *relaxes again.*] It's ruined. You can all say. I'm not sensitive. I look terrible.

LESLEY: It's beautiful.

HAROLD: You look gorgeous!

[*Which is roughly the sentence* RITA'S *been waiting for since she got home.*]

RITA: Emess?

HAROLD: Emess.

RITA: Victor?

[VICTOR'S *too busy pigging himself to hear.*] Victor.

VICTOR: Hello?

RITA: What do you think?

VICTOR: What about?

RITA: Your honest opinion. You hate it. I don't mind.

VICTOR: Good. I don't even know what you're talking about!

RITA: My hair.

VICTOR [*shrugs*]: What can I say? It's hair.

RITA: Do you like it?

VICTOR: It's done *me* no harm.

HAROLD [*to* RITA, *immediately stepping into the breach*]: I've never seen it look so nice.

RITA: Emess?

LESLEY: He's said Emess once!

HAROLD: Emess.

RITA: Good. [*A tiny pause.*] She's coming first thing in the morning to give it a comb out. I'll ask her to take out the streaks.

HAROLD: That's what so beautiful! The streaks!

[*Which is* exactly *the sentence she's been waiting to hear since she got home.*]

RITA: Well, in that case . . .

[*From time to time during the above dialogue, we see* ELIOT *watching the others – particularly* VICTOR *and* HAROLD *– carefully, expressionlessly. A silence. They eat.*]

17. Int. Living room.

[*The family as before. They're now in the middle of the main course.*]

LESLEY [*tentatively*]: Dinner O.K., everyone? Any complaints?

HAROLD: Fantastic. Really fantastic. Great.

LESLEY: Well . . . if one gets food-poisoning, we all will. Mum? Nice?

HAROLD: A banquet. Straight up. Tremendous.

LESLEY: Mum?

RITA: Lovely, darling. [*A beat.*] You didn't warm the brisket on too high a light you don't think?

LESLEY [*stung*]: It doesn't taste burnt!

RITA: No, no. It's nice . . . Crispy . . . different.

LESLEY: Dad?

VICTOR: What?

RITA: Lesley wanted to know – nice dinner?

VICTOR: The whole bloody family's gone pot-shop! It's like a dinner – I'm eating it! Harold, you think she's wonderful, what's she hakking me on a kop for?

[*Silence for a moment, as they eat. Then, suddenly,* RITA *clatters her knife and fork down. Startled, they all look at her.*]

RITA: Stan and Dora Clyne!

LESLEY: What about them?

RITA: They didn't RSVP! We don't know if they're coming to the dinner-dance! Victor!

VICTOR: If they come, they come. If they don't, they don't. Confucius Cohen. [*To* LESLEY] Pass the salt.

[HAROLD *immediately reaches over to pass the salt to* VICTOR.]

RITA: The seating plan, though! It'll make ashenblotty of the seating plan! They should be on the second table and it's full!

LESLEY: They're not relations.

RITA: He's a doctor. He expects it. [*Sighs.*] They'll give him a beautiful present.

LESLEY: They may not be coming!

RITA [*worriedly*]: By the same token . . .

VICTOR: Rita. Let me eat.

RITA: You'd think they'd RSVP. A man in his position . . .

VICTOR: Perhaps they didn't get the invitation. Perhaps they were in Bournemouth. He's a doctor, perhaps he can't read decent writing. Perhaps he couldn't afford a stamp – who can?

[*A brief pause.*]

RITA [*almost to herself*]: It was stamped already. It was a stamped-addressed card. No expense spared.

VICTOR: Rita. For the first time in three months may I eat without hearing seating-plans and menus and caterers and do we tip the rabbi and should we invite Miriam and what if it rains and shall I wear a long dress or a short and nothing'll spoil it, will it? In the morning, he gets bar mitzvah'd. In the evening we have the dinner-

dance. By Sunday – it's all a dream. Thank you. Amen.
[ELIOT *has been watching them closely, throughout.*
They eat for a moment in silence.]

18. Int. Living room.

[*The family as before.* RITA *is serving them with fruit salad or fruit.*
A moment's silence.]

RITA: Do you think we should give her a bouquet? Not too dear?

LESLEY: Who?

RITA: Mrs Sherman.

VICTOR: Is she anyone we know?

RITA: The rabbi's wife.

VICTOR: *Certainly* give her a bouquet! I've never met the woman! Give everybody a bouquet! Plant trees for them in Israel! It's already costing me three insurance policies! [*Sighs.*] Roll on Sunday.

RITA [*gravely*]: You want it over with? The greatest honour of your life?

VICTOR: You know what I mean.

RITA: I'm afraid I don't. Do *you* know what he means, Harold?

HAROLD: Um ... well, in a sense ... um ... [*he looks, trapped, from one to the other.*] ... well, yes and no. What he, in my view, well, *doesn't* mean is –

VICTOR [*wearily*]: She knows what I mean. She knows what I mean when *I* don't.

[*A silence. They all eat (except* ELIOT).
VICTOR *turns to* ELIOT.]

Hey, Blabbermouth. You going to practise your speech tonight?

ELIOT: Yes.

RITA: He'll practise his speech like he went for a haircut.

LESLEY: Didn't you like your dinner?

ELIOT: Terrific.

LESLEY: Apart from not eating it.

ELIOT: I wasn't hungry.

RITA: No, because you've been nashing all afternoon, haven't you? I'm going to put a lock on that fridge. And tomorrow morning before we go to shul, you get that hair cut.

VICTOR: There won't be time.

RITA: Victor, he's not standing in a beautiful synagogue on the greatest day of his life, looking like Kojak.

[*They all stare at her, puzzled.*]

LESLEY: Kojak's *bald*.

RITA [*evasively*]: Not Kojak. The other one.

LESLEY: *Which* other one??

RITA [*even more evasively*]: She picks me up on every little thing . . .

VICTOR: Lesley, leave your mother alone. Harold, you think she's wonderful, tell her to leave her mother alone.

RITA [*to* LESLEY, *angrily*]: If *I* don't do the worrying, who will?

LESLEY: *Now* what's she on about?

VICTOR [*to* ELIOT]: See! Satisfied?

ELIOT [*suddenly*]: I thought it was a *bar mitzvah* tomorrow!

[*They all stare at him, shocked at his abrupt outburst.*]

I thought I was supposed to read the blessings, and the portion of the law and be the guest of honour at the dinner-dance. The Torah doesn't mention it's a hair-dressing contest!

[*An uncomfortable pause. Exchanged glances.*]

VICTOR [*quietly*]: Look. Everybody just eat. All week I'm in bloody traffic jams. Just eat.

[*A silence. They eat.*]

HAROLD: Here. I've got a cracker for you. You'll appreciate this one. There's this Yiddishe feller –

VICTOR: Always has to be a Yiddishe feller, have you noticed? Can't be a Chinaman or a bloody Eskimo.

HAROLD [*puzzled*]: But it's a Yiddishe story!

LESLEY [*annoyed with* VICTOR]: Go on, Harold. Please him. 'There's this Eskimo and his son's getting bar mitzvah'd ...'

VICTOR: He didn't say it was about a bar mitzvah!

LESLEY: Who can say anything with you jumping down their throat!

VICTOR [*relenting*]: All right, all right. There's this Yiddishe feller ...

HAROLD: ... and his son's getting bar mitzvah'd – or going to. And the feller's a multi-millionaire, right? Could buy and sell Tesco's and still have change in his pocket. So, off he goes to the caterers and –

RITA: Did you ring them, Lesley?

LESLEY: Who? No. Shush.

HAROLD: ... And he says to the caterer, he says, 'Listen, I'm not short of a bob or two. For my kid I want the best bar mitzvah there's ever been. But the best. Something different. Something nobody else has ever had. The cream. What've you got?' So the caterer says, 'Mr Whateveritis,' he says – Schlomberg, Picklebaum ... whatever ...

LESLEY: Go on!

HAROLD: 'Have I got a bar mitzvah for you! Unique. Never been done before. How many guests you want to invite?' 'A thousand,' he says.

RITA [*worriedly, to herself*]: God help him!

HAROLD: So the caterer says 'All right Mr Picklebaum – or Shishelkop or whatever – '

LESLEY: Go on!

HAROLD: 'All right, sir, this is what you do. You send invitations to all your guests to meet at London Airport. And they've *no idea* where they're going. They all get in a jumbo jet – bingo! – straight to Africa. They get out, there's a white Rolls-Royce each waiting for them on the tarmac. One each, chauffeur-driven. They drive through the beautiful scenery. Marvellous. Seen nothing like it.

They get to the edge of the jungle, out of the Rolls-Royces, on to an elephant each. Each elephant covered in gold and silver, and a little Sabu on top driving.

So. Off they go, into the jungle – a thousand guests on a thousand elephants. Through the jungle, three days and nights, stopping at the best kosher hotels, till finally, on the last night – bingo! – there's this dirty great clearing in the middle of the jungle! And there all the tables are set out, waiters from the Savoy, dance floor, the rabbi, the bar mitzvah boy, you and your good lady wife, Ivy Benson and her Band, smoked salmon, the lot! The greatest banquet in the history of Man. Two million quid, wholesale.' And the feller says, 'I like it,' he says, 'It's different. You're on!'

So. Time for the kid's bar mitzvah. Off they all go to London Airport. Jumbo jet. Rolls-Royce each. Elephant each. Time of their lives. Into the jungle. First day. Second day. And on the third day, they're all plodding along in single file down this narrow trail, when the guide on the front elephant suddenly peers through the jungle – there's a thousand elephants plodding towards him one after the other! 'Everybody stop!' he shouts, 'Our bloody mazel – there's another bar mitzvah coming this way!'

[HAROLD's *joke goes down like a cast-iron cannonball.* LESLEY – *who's heard it before and loves it – laughs loyally. The others, preoccupied for their different reasons, with tomorrow's bar mitzvah, see nothing funny in it at all. An embarrassed pause.*]

LESLEY [*annoyed*]: It's good! It's a good joke!
RITA [*starting to gather up the used dishes, absently*]: I'll give Stan and Dora a ring later on. In case they're crainked. One less thing to go wrong.
[*Fade to black.*]

27

19. Int. Kitchen.

[HAROLD, *wearing an apron, is washing up the dinner plates.* ELIOT *slouches in aimlessly, picks up a leftover bit of carrot from one of the plates and nibbles at it. He sits down and concentrates, solemnly, on watching* HAROLD *working.* HAROLD *feels discomfited by his silent staring.*]

HAROLD: All right, then?

ELIOT: Pardon?

HAROLD: Everything all right?

ELIOT: Yes, thanks.

HAROLD: Just sort of sitting staring a bit, are you?

ELIOT: I thought that was a woman's job? Or is that just a theory put about by chauvinist pigs?

HAROLD [*defensively*]: It happens to be a special occasion, doesn't it? Everybody else is busy driving each other barmy, aren't they?

[ELIOT *sits, unmoved, impassive, watching him.*]

ELIOT: You *always* do it. Always. Toujours. Semper.

HAROLD: 'Always'?? I can hardly do it *always*. I only come here Fridays. 'Always,' he says . . .

[*A pause.*]

ELIOT: Always on Fridays you do it.

[HAROLD *grows more uncomfortable.*]
My dad never does it.

HAROLD: No, well, your dad's . . . [*Checks himself.*] . . . your dad, isn't he? [*Brief pause.*] I've seen him dry them once or twice.

ELIOT: They're even wetter after he dries. He does it badly on purpose.

[LESLEY *races in, wearing an inflated hairdryer-bag on her head. She crosses to pick up her handbag from the table.*]

LESLEY: No one talk to me. I can't hear.

[*She picks up the handbag and starts to exit.* HAROLD

28

mouths an affectionate kiss at her. She very automatically
mouths a brief peck back, and exits busily.
ELIOT watches the little exchange, deadpan.
HAROLD continues washing up.]

HAROLD [suddenly brusque]: Look, haven't you things to do!
A million. You must have.

ELIOT: She doesn't appreciate it, you know.

HAROLD: You've your speech to learn, two lots of Hebrew,
the blessings . . .

ELIOT: You think it's a mating-call, don't you – washing-
up? No other species of animals do it. You don't see
giraffes washing up for female giraffes. She won't suddenly show you her knickers etcetera.

HAROLD [angry]: All right, Eliot. Go and be comical else-
where, O.K.?

ELIOT: O.K. [starts to go.]

HAROLD [angry]: It's manners, isn't it! I'm thanking your
parents for their hospitality! It's a nice thing to do,
pleasing people!

[ELIOT exits, paying him no attention.]

20. Int. Hallway.

[ELIOT wanders out of the kitchen towards the living room. In
passing, he buries the remnant of his leftover carrot in the soil of a
flowerpot.]

21. Int. Living room.

[VICTOR is slouched in an easy chair watching television –
arrested in the middle of polishing his shoes for tomorrow.
RITA is seated at the (cleared) table, with a pencil and a sheet of
paper on which is an itemized list.
ELIOT wanders in and flops into an armchair. He looks from one

to the other a couple of times. They ignore him: VICTOR *pre-occupied with the TV programme,* RITA *with her list.*]

RITA [*reading*]: 'In morning: One – no "maybe" about it, ring caterers. Two: everyone get ready for shul. Three: no one put best clothes on till after breakfast.' [*She looks up agitatedly.*] Victor!

VICTOR [*eyes never leaving the TV screen throughout*]: Hello?

RITA: Will you *help* me!

VICTOR: Doing what?

RITA: Showing *interest*!

VICTOR: I'm showing! I'm showing!

RITA: It's everything we do! If we're going on holiday . . . If we're getting the decorators . . . whatever needs doing – me, always me . . . if we need a plumber –

VICTOR: All right, all right! I'm watching something. I can talk while I'm watching.

[RITA *returns irritatedly to her list.*]

RITA [*reading*]: 'Four: Sylvia to give my hair comb-out.' [*She glances at* ELIOT.] 'Four A: ask Sylvia to give Eliot quick haircut . . .'

VICTOR [*watching TV*]: If time.

RITA: If time.

VICTOR [*watching TV*]: There won't be.

RITA: 'Five: set off to synagogue.' [*A new worry suddenly strikes her. She wheels round to* VICTOR *again.*] Is there petrol in the car? We're not sitting in a garage getting petrol in our best clothes, Victor!

VICTOR [*watching TV*]: There's petrol. There's petrol.

ELIOT [*quietly*]: I thought we weren't supposed to drive on the Sabbath. I thought it was a sin.

[*No response from either of them.*]

I thought we were supposed to walk.

VICTOR: All right, all right, you've made your point!

ELIOT: I thought that was covered by the Fourth Commandment: remember the Sabbath Day to keep it holy.

VICTOR: So we'll park a couple of streets from the shul and walk the rest, terrible thing! We won't be seen.

ELIOT: Won't we?

RITA: All the congregation do it.

ELIOT: I wasn't thinking of the congregation.

RITA: Well, other people couldn't care less, could they!

ELIOT: I wasn't thinking of other people.

RITA: Eliot, can you try and sit in the chair like a normal human being? Is it too much to ask? Dralon grows on trees?

[ELIOT *rearranges himself on the chair.*]

[*Reading from her list*] 'Six: after the service return to —'

ELIOT [*to* VICTOR]: Any good?

VICTOR: What?

[ELIOT *nods towards the TV set.*]

I've seen it before.

[*He nevertheless continues watching with avid attention.*

RITA *promptly gets up, crosses to the TV set, switches it off and returns to her chair and her list.*]

Thank you. Twelve quid a year licence fee, I pay . . .

RITA [*reading*]: 'Seven: as soon as he's home, Eliot change clothes, hang suit up in wardrobe ready for evening —'

[*She sees* ELIOT *taking a toffee from a sweet dish.*]

If you're hungry why didn't you eat your dinner?

ELIOT: I'm not.

RITA: Well, why are you eating sweets and taking the enamel off your teeth?

ELIOT: I'm not. I'm just unwrapping it.

RITA: What for?

[*A pause, while* ELIOT *tries to think of an excuse that could possibly sound plausible.*]

ELIOT: It's a new hobby.

RITA [*reading*]: 'Eight: ring caterers —'

[*The front doorbell rings.*]

VICTOR: Eliot, let your grandad in.

ELIOT: I thought I'd go and learn my speech.

VICTOR: Like all of a sudden! Let him in *then* learn it!

[ELIOT *levers himself from the chair and starts to wander towards the door.*]

RITA [*to* VICTOR, re *the list*]: Can you think of anything I've missed out?

VICTOR: No.

RITA: I didn't see you think!

VICTOR: There was nothing to *see*! I'm an invisible thinker.

22. Int. Hallway.

[HAROLD, *drying his hands on his apron, has beaten* ELIOT *to the front door, and is ingratiatingly admitting* ELIOT'S GRAN-DAD, *Mr Wax*.]

HAROLD [*effusively*]: Good shabbos, Mr Wax!

[GRANDAD *is slightly disappointed that it's only* HAROLD *that's opened the door*.]

GRANDAD: Shabbos. And how's the finest solicitor you could wish for?

HAROLD: Accountant. Fine, Mr Wax, and how's your back?

[GRANDAD *is happily diverted by the sight of* ELIOT *lurking further down the hall*.]

GRANDAD: There he is! The bar mitzvah boy! [*He totters towards* ELIOT.] How's the loveliest grandson you could wish for? [*He hugs the reluctant* ELIOT *and pinches his cheek*.] I could eat him!

ELIOT: Hello, Zaidy.

GRANDAD: 'Hello,' he says! So beautiful I could eat him! Bless his little pipick!

[*Cut to see* LESLEY *on her way downstairs* (*still wearing her hairdryer*). *On seeing her grandfather, she shudders to a halt, and tries to creep back up again, unseen. Too late.*]

Lesley!

LESLEY: No one talk. I can't hear.

GRANDAD: A kiss for your Zaidy! How's the most ravishing granddaughter you could wish for? A bathing beauty!

[*Sighingly, she comes downstairs for her Friday kiss. He kisses smackingly, she briefly.*]

Such a film star she's grown! How long since I've seen you?

LESLEY: Last Friday. Must go. Armpits to shave. [*She makes her way back upstairs.*]

HAROLD: Shall I take your coat, Mr Wax?

GRANDAD: A gentleman.

[*He allows* HAROLD *to divest him of his coat.*

ELIOT *uses the diversion to try and escape upstairs. Too late.*]

Hey! Young man! Bar mitzvah boy! You're not coming to sit on your Zaidy's knee?

ELIOT: I've to learn my speech and my Hebrew and my ten commandments.

GRANDAD [*satisfied*]: I could eat him!

[*He goes into the living room.*

HAROLD *returns to the kitchen.*

ELIOT *lingers on the stairs, then returns a couple of steps to eavesdrop.*]

[*O.O.V. in living room*] Don't get up, don't get up! I'll have a cup of tea and a piece of sponge-cake – but only if *you're* having. Good shabbos.

RITA [*O.O.V.*]: Shabbos, dad.

VICTOR [*O.O.V.*]: Shabbos, Chaim. How's your back?

GRANDAD [*O.O.V.*]: Who cares? So I keep the doctors in work. Listen.

[*This is the moment* ELIOT *has been lurking for. He mouths each word of the following, in perfect mime with* GRANDAD'S *voice.*]

If the kids are happy, you're happy. If you're happy, I'm happy. If you're all happy, thank God, I'm the happiest man in the world. It's my happiness – what should I do, cry?

[ELIOT *continues upstairs.*]

23. Int. Bathroom.

[LESLEY *is taking the curlers from her hair before the mirror.*
ELIOT *slouches in. He sits on the edge of the bath and watches her.*]

LESLEY: Go on. Some cutting remark regarded as brilliant in the B Stream.

ELIOT: I wasn't going to say *anything*. Nothing. Rien. Nihil.

LESLEY: Good!

[*A beat.*]

ELIOT: What do you think of Harold?

[LESLEY *gives him a sharp, apprehensive glance.*]

LESLEY: What do you mean 'What do I think of Harold?'

ELIOT: What do you think of him?

LESLEY: We're nearly engaged, aren't we!

ELIOT: That's no answer.

LESLEY: Is the back of my hand an answer?

ELIOT: Do you *reckon* him?

LESLEY: We're nearly bloody engaged!!

[*A short pause.*]

ELIOT: Do you reckon Dad?

LESLEY: Dad??

ELIOT: Dad.

LESLEY: Well ... well, he's *dad*, isn't he! What's got into you?

ELIOT: And do you reckon grandad?

LESLEY: Of course!

ELIOT: Why? Pourquoi? Cur?

LESLEY [*drily*]: Sorry, I missed the English one.

ELIOT: 'Why'.

LESLEY: Why what?

ELIOT: Why do you reckon them?

LESLEY: Well, that's a particularly stupid question, isn't it? Even from you!

ELIOT [*quietly*]: You must be man-*mad*. [*He promptly exits,*

34

then just as promptly pops his head back in.] What about *me*?
LESLEY: What *about* you?
    [*He exits again.*
    LESLEY *watches him go. She dismisses her edginess and returns to her curler-removing.*]

24. Int. Eliot's bedroom.

[ELIOT *is lying on his bed, hands clasped behind his head. The following speech may be spoken directly, or voice-over.*]

ELIOT: My dear mother and father, my dear sister, my dear grandfather, Rabbi Sherman, relatives and friends. On this day that marks my passage from boyhood to manhood, I would like to thank you all for the great honour you have bestowed on me by your presence at this dinner-dance. I shall cherish it all my life without fail. I would like to thank Rabbi Sherman also for the patience he has bestowed on me during the last year while preparing me to learn the portion of the law which I had the honour to recite in the synagogue today. He has been no end of a tower of strength in no uncertain terms. Most of all I would like to thank my dear mother and father for the guidance, wisdom and love which they have bestowed on me during my boyhood.

Now that I am a Man, I will follow my dear father's example, and that of my dear grandfather, and last but not least that of my sister Lesley's boyfriend, Harold, in living my life with truth, industry and selfless devotion according to the moral teachings of the Talmud. At the risk of repeating myself, they have been no end of a tower of strength in no uncertain terms. I sincerely hope that I will be a credit to them all, and that they will say of me, as Antony did of Brutus in Act 5, scene 5, line 73, 'This was a Man'. Thank you all for the wonderful presents you have bestowed on me of which I am extremely grateful for. I trust you will enjoy your evening, not forgetting the dancing which is about to ensue, as I feel sure you assuredly will. Thank you.

25. Int. Living room.

[*Empty cups, remnants of sponge-cake in evidence.*
VICTOR *and* HAROLD, *seated in armchairs, are in the middle of a growingly-heated discussion.*
GRANDAD, *in his armchair, nods wisely in agreement with each point made . . . however conflicting they are.*]

VICTOR: 'They'd a right to march'??? 'They'd a right to march'????

HAROLD [*uncomfortably*]: They'd a right to march. It's legal.

VICTOR: Legal?

HAROLD: Of course it's legal!

VICTOR: So's pneumonia.

HAROLD [*baffled*]: Pneumonia?

VICTOR: It doesn't make it desirable, does it! Blocking up all the streets, waving their banners, traffic held up for miles . . .

HAROLD: Yes, well, that's unfortunate . . . unfortunately.

VICTOR: Oh, is it? Twenty minutes I was held up, mate! With an empty bloody cab! Do you know how much that comes to on the clock? You're the accountant round here!

HAROLD: All I'm saying is they've a right to campaign for better working conditions. You're the trade unionist!

VICTOR: And proud of it, sonny boy!

HAROLD: Well then!

VICTOR: Well what?

GRANDAD [*carefully, slowly, with consummate wisdom*]: Listen The way I look at it . . . call me an intellectual if you must . . . everybody should make just enough to be comfortable. Then be satisfied. In that way, there's no marches, no strikes, and everybody's happy. That's my solution. But my mazel, I'm not Prime Minister.

[*They both stare at him, nonplussed. A tiny pause, then they return to their argument as though he'd never spoken.*]

VICTOR: Go on . . . I'm a trade unionist . . .

HAROLD: *I'm* the true blue! They're *your* brothers!

VICTOR: *I'm* my brother, mate! *Me!*

26. Int. Eliot's bedroom.

[ELIOT *gets his Hebrew books out, and opens them. He hears the argument continuing downstairs, and closes his books again. He lies on the bed listening. The door is open.*]

VICTOR [*O.O.V.*]: You'd give in to *all* of them!

HAROLD [*O.O.V.*]: Excuse me, credit where it's due . . . it
• was me that was against the miners and railwaymen!

VICTOR [*O.O.V.*]: Yes. Typical.

HAROLD [*O.O.V.*]: You're not even agreeing with your own party!

VICTOR [*O.O.V.*]: Nor are you!

HAROLD [*O.O.V.*]: Just because you personally lost twenty minutes' work . . .

VICTOR [*O.O.V.*]: How you can be a Tory beats me. You're not supposed to feel sorry for people, Harold. You're not supposed to *care* about working conditions. You'd get drummed out of the *Communists, you* would!

HAROLD [*O.O.V.*]: Now you sound like Sir Keith Joseph!

27. Int. Living room.

[VICTOR, HAROLD, GRANDAD . . . *as before, the discussion continuing.*]

VICTOR: *He* beats me altogether. A Yiddishe feller. When I was a lad, they gave you your Labour Party member-

ship card the minute you were circumcised. Give you
with one hand, take away with the other ...

GRANDAD: Listen.

> [*They listen.*]

The way I look at it ... [*as though no one's ever thought of it
before.*] ... there's good and bad in everybody!

> [*A long pause.*]

VICTOR: Oh, I see.

GRANDAD: I believe they should all be happy.

> [*A pause.*]

VICTOR: Yes, Chaim.

GRANDAD: You prefer I should want them to be *unhappy*?

VICTOR: Do you want everybody to get higher wages?

GRANDAD: I do.

HAROLD: Even if the country can't afford it?

GRANDAD: I'd *like* the country to afford it.

VICTOR: And what if it can't?

GRANDAD: You wanted my opinion, you got it. There are
two sides to every story, Victor.

VICTOR: Right! Well, whose side are you *on*!!

GRANDAD [*with consummate wisdom*]:

> Our entry to it is naked and bare,
> Our journey through it is trouble and care,
> Our exit from it is God knows where,
> So if we're all right here,
> We're all right there.

28. Int. Parents' bedroom.

[RITA *and* LESLEY *are taking the dry-cleaned clothes from their
cellophaned wrappings and laying them carefully on the bed.*]

RITA: Made a beautiful job of them, haven't they?

LESLEY [*not interested*]: Very nice.

RITA: Perfect. [*She picks up* VICTOR's *perfectly-creased
trousers.*] I'll put a new crease in your dad's trousers.

LESLEY: They've just come from the cleaners!!
RITA: I know.
LESLEY: You said they were perfect!
RITA: I like a crease to be a crease, I can't help it. It's my nature. I'll do them while I'm doing Eliot's.

29. Int. Eliot's bedroom.

[ELIOT, *still lying on his bed, is listening to* RITA *and* LESLEY.]

ELIOT [*calling*]: Mine haven't even come from the cleaners. Mine are *new*! It's a new suit. They don't *need* pressing.

30. Int. Parents' bedroom.

[RITA *and* LESLEY *as before.*]

RITA [*calling back*]: For Burton's *window*, they don't need pressing. [*To* LESLEY] Which tie do you think for your dad? [*She holds up several ties.*] Not for *me*, you notice. But I have to choose. He'd rather sit on his behind watching television and arguing. Me – I have the headaches . . .
LESLEY: Me – I have the cold sores . . .
RITA: Mmm?
LESLEY: I didn't speak.
RITA: You said *something*.
LESLEY: I was singing.
RITA: Which tie?
LESLEY [*not interested*]: The brown one.
RITA: The brown?
LESLEY: The brown.

31. Int. Eliot's bedroom.

[ELIOT – *listening as before*.]

RITA [*O.O.V.*]: He's already worn the brown. At Micky Fisher's wedding. Everybody else in evening dress of course . . .

LESLEY [*O.O.V. wearily*]: Not the brown. Any. The blue.

RITA [*O.O.V.*]: 'Any,' she says. Thank you. A splitting headache I've had for six months – she says 'any' . . .

VICTOR [*O.O.V., calling*]: Rita, Chaim's going now!

RITA [*O.O.V., calling*]: See you tomorrow, Pop. Mind the roads. God bless.

GRANDAD [*O.O.V., calling*]: God bless.

LESLEY [*O.O.V., calling*]: Cheerio, Zaidy!

GRANDAD [*O.O.V., calling*]: You going to be the belle of the ball tomorrow, please God?

LESLEY [*O.O.V., calling*]: Who else?

GRANDAD [*O.O.V.*]: Beautiful she is!

VICTOR [*O.O.V., calling*]: Eliot! Grandad's going now!

ELIOT [*calling*]: 'Night, Zaidy!

GRANDAD [*O.O.V., calling*]: Do I get a big kiss from the loveliest boy you could wish for?

ELIOT [*calling*]: I'm just studying at the moment, Zaidy. [*He opens a book and flips the pages over loudly, then closes it again.*]

GRANDAD [*O.O.V.*]: A leben on his kishkes! I could eat him! See you tomorrow, everybody!

[*Short, reciprocal mumbled farewells from* VICTOR, RITA, HAROLD *and* LESLEY.

We hear the front door open, then close.]

32. Int. Hallway.

[LESLEY *is seeing* HAROLD *off at the door.* HAROLD *is reluctant to go and affectionate.* LESLEY, *to her credit, is trying hard not to appear as though she's trying to get rid of him. Which she is.*]

LESLEY: Night, night, then love.

HAROLD: I've hardly seen you all evening. Let alone had half a chance to . . . [*He moves tenderly towards her.*]

LESLEY [*pulling back slightly*]: Be different once tomorrow's over with. Sunday, we'll be back to normal. If it ever comes.

HAROLD [*smiling hopefully*]: Will I see you Sunday then?

LESLEY: Oh, hell! I promised Valerie I'd go round to tell her Sidney isn't the be-all and end-all and she's better off without him. That'll take all day.

HAROLD [*disappointed*]: Oh.

LESLEY: Anyway, we'll see each other tomorrow!

HAROLD: Not . . . well, not just the two of us . . .

LESLEY: No. A hundred and seventeen.

[*He moves to snuggle his face against hers. She pulls back slightly.*]

Ah!

HAROLD: What?

LESLEY: Hair!

HAROLD [*pulling back*]: Sorry.

[*He moves to take her hand. She pulls it back.*]

LESLEY: Oops! Nail varnish!

[*They stand for a moment. He smiles.*]

HAROLD: Well, thanks for dinner.

LESLEY: Pleasure, Harold.

HAROLD: Fantastic.

[*Cut to see* ELIOT *emerging from the bathroom in his pyjamas. He sees* LESLEY *and* HAROLD *at the doorway and stops to lean over the banister and watch.*]

As long as I was of some help . . .

LESLEY: Help?

HAROLD [*diffidently*]: Well . . . washing up, not that it's any trouble . . . and polishing Eliot's shoes for tomorrow . . . and one of your dad's . . . I mean it's all family, isn't it, or soon will be . . . putting the dishes away . . . I don't mind, it's no trouble to me . . . making the tea, fetching the sponge-cake . . .

LESLEY: You're very sweet.

HAROLD: Am I?

[*He moves to kiss her. She immediately looks at her watch.*]

LESLEY: Hey! What about my beauty sleep then?

[*He pulls back.*]

HAROLD: Sorry.

LESLEY: Don't apologize.

HAROLD: Sorry.

LESLEY: Harold!!

HAROLD: 'Night, then.

LESLEY: G'night.

HAROLD: Love you.

LESLEY: Love *you*.

[*They mouth a kiss at each other and* HAROLD *exits.*
LESLEY *closes the door and locks it.*
Cut to ELIOT *watching her as she goes back to the living room. He stands for a moment, then suddenly goes into a frenetic, but silent, monkey impersonation, pulling a face and scratching under his arms. Then, just as abruptly, he stops and returns to his usual solemn demeanour.*]

ELIOT [*calling*]: Goodnight, everyone.

[*From different rooms we hear* VICTOR, RITA *and* LESLEY *call 'goodnight'.*]

33. Int. Parents' bedroom.

[RITA *and* VICTOR *are in bed. The room is in darkness, lit slightly by moonlight.*
They speak gently and quietly throughout the scene. Both in a mood totally different from what we've seen them in so far.

42

They lie on their backs, facing the ceiling.
RITA *is wearing an elaborate hairnet to protect her hairdo.*]

RITA: Well . . . all over bar the whatisit.

VICTOR: Shouting.

RITA: Shouting.

VICTOR: Now give the worrying a rest, kid.

RITA: Yes.

VICTOR: This time tomorrow night it'll all be history.

RITA: Harold's promised to take colour photographs.

VICTOR: Cine.

RITA: Mmm?

VICTOR: Cine. Eight millimetre.

RITA: I knew it was something. [*Sigh.*] Anyway, I'll give the worrying a rest.

VICTOR: That's the idea.

RITA: I can't think of anything I've missed out.

VICTOR: No.

RITA: I've taken a valium.

VICTOR: Good.

   [*A pause.*]

RITA: Eliot's been in a funny mood.

VICTOR: Nerves. Funny age. Only natural.

RITA [*not completely convinced*]: Yes. [*Pause.*] Have you got butterflies?

VICTOR: No. A few. Who's counting.

RITA: You can have some of mine. I bet I cry all day tomorrow. I'm taking six hankies just in case. *New* ones. I've been saving them.

   [*Pause.*]

VICTOR: Where the hell thirteen years go to, eh? Thirteen years. Now you see 'em, now you don't. Skinny little kid rubbing poached egg in the carpet. Punkt! It can't be more than five minutes since I bought him a scooter for being vaccinated.

RITA: That was *Lesley.*

VICTOR: Good God, was it?

43

RITA: For going to the dentist's.

[*Pause.*]

VICTOR: You'll never need six hankies.

RITA: *You'll* need *five* of them.

[*A gentle laugh.*]

Not done too bad, have we, all told? Since our Bethnal Green days.

VICTOR: Not bad.

RITA: You never used to go to shul on a Saturday in them days. West Ham *United*, yes.

VICTOR: Well ... different world, then. [*Pause.*] Everything different. I sometimes wonder if *I* was a different feller ... someone else altogether ...

RITA [*matter-of-factly*]: I don't think so ...

VICTOR: I've thought of an element of humour for my speech at the dinner. 'In conclusion, may I say that for a father his son's bar mitzvah is the most beautiful service seen in a synagogue.'

RITA: Very nice.

VICTOR: 'Not that I go all that much.'

RITA: You're not saying that?

VICTOR: 'For as Rabbi Sherman once said to me ... I don't often see you in the synagogue very often, Mr Green. And as I replied ... I don't often see you driving a cab very often, Rabbi Sherman.'

RITA: You can't say that!

VICTOR: Then, wait for laughter to die down, and I say 'But *today* I wouldn't have missed for the world. Thank you.'

[*A pause.*]

RITA: Funny, isn't it? It'll be like happy and sad at the same time.

VICTOR: Well, that's what growing up is, isn't it? Bit of a laugh, bit of a cry ...

RITA [*pause*]: Everything'll go all right. I can't think why it shouldn't – we'll be dressed up – we'll look very smart.

34. Int. Eliot's bedroom.

[*The room is in half-darkness.*
ELIOT *is in bed, seemingly asleep.*
The door opens and LESLEY *enters, wearing a nightdress.*]

LESLEY [*whispering tentatively*]: Are you asleep?
ELIOT: Yes.
LESLEY: Can I come in?
ELIOT: No.
      [*She comes in and sits on the side of the bed.*]
LESLEY: Hello, Horrible.
ELIOT: Shouldn't you be having your beauty sleep? Or have you given up hope?
LESLEY: Hey, how'd you like every evening to be like that one?
ELIOT: Not a lot.
      [LESLEY *smiles.*]
LESLEY: How was school today?
ELIOT: All right.
LESLEY: Did Squidge find out who nicked his pocket-calculator?
ELIOT: He thinks it was Expletive-Deleted.
LESLEY: Who??
ELIOT: The maths teacher.
      [*A pause – then the reason she's come to see him.*]
LESLEY: Are you all right, our kid?
ELIOT: Yes, thanks. Merci. Gratias.
LESLEY: It always happens. The panic. Even in normal families. It's a big day for them. The biggest in their lives. Bigger than it is for *you* in a way. Soon be over.
ELIOT: Yes.
LESLEY: You get some sleep then. And don't lie there thinking about it. And no dreaming, either. By order. Except football or cricket or Olivia Newton-John. Is it Olivia Newton-John these days?

ELIOT: Suzie Quatro.

LESLEY: Suzie Quatro then. [*She gets up.*] See you in the morning, mate.

ELIOT: See you.

[*She exits.*

ELIOT lies for a moment, seemingly near to tears. He then very quietly gets out of bed and starts replacing his posters on the wall, and his toys and books back on the shelves.

Fade to black.]

35. Ext. Synagogue. Saturday morning.

[RABBI SHERMAN *is walking briskly along the street towards the synagogue. He reaches the entrance and goes in.*]

36. Int. Synagogue.

[WILFRED, *the caretaker, is placing prayer-books along the pews. The door opens and* RABBI SHERMAN, *still wearing hat and coat, pops his head in.*]

RABBI: Morning, Wilfred. Good shabbos.

WILFRED: Morning, Rabbi Sherman.

RABBI: Have you had a cup of coffee?

WILFRED: There was only one spoonful. I finished it off. I didn't think.

RABBI: No, no, fine. I wasn't hinting.

WILFRED: No, I know.

RABBI: I *meant* had *you* had.

WILFRED: Yes, I know.

37. Int. Living room.

[*The nervous panic of the previous evening is now rapidly reaching its peak.*

RITA, *in her best dress, is seated on a hardbacked chair, while* SYLVIA *gives her hair the promised comb-out.*

VICTOR, *in his best suit, is standing having his tie properly knotted by* LESLEY, *in her best dress. Though still in his shirt sleeves, holding his jacket by its hanger,* VICTOR *is already wearing his bowler hat.*

RITA *has the phone-cradle in her lap. She's speaking into the phone.*]

RITA: Hello, Levy's? Levy's the Caterers? Good morning, Mrs Green speaking. May I speak to Mr Levy, please? [*She feels her hair tugged by the comb.*] Ow!

SYLVIA: You want to be beautiful, you have to suffer a little, it's human nature, I apologize.

RITA: My fault. [*Brief pause.*] Victor, your lace is undone.

VICTOR: I *like* it undone.

RITA [*calling*]: Eliot! Are you ready? We're moving out of the house *now*! We're on the doorstep! [*Brief pause.*] I'm not sure about that colour eyeshadow, Lesley, but then I'm not Mary Quant.

LESLEY: And, then again, you're not wearing it. [*To* VICTOR] Keep still.

VICTOR: 'Keep still'? I'm keeping still. What am I doing? The four hundred metres hurdles? I'm keeping still.

LESLEY: All right, all right.

VICTOR: What am I doing? The four hundred metres hurdles or something?

RITA [*into phone*]: Hello? Mr Levy? Good morning, Mrs Green speaking. Just ringing to say hello really.

[*Pause.* VICTOR *and* LESLEY *exchange a glance.*]
No, nothing . . . Just that my husband wanted to know if everything was in order.
[*A dirty look from* VICTOR.]

47

No, no, *certainly* there's no reason it shouldn't be. [*Pause.*]
Yes, yes I'll tell him. Thank you. Good shabbos. [*She hangs
up and yells.*] Eliot! Your dad's starting the car!

[*By now,* VICTOR *and* LESLEY *have their coats and hats on.*
VICTOR *is busy with the clothes-brush;* LESLEY *is re-
applying lipstick.*]

VICTOR: Tell me what?

RITA: What?

VICTOR: 'Yes, I'll tell him,' you said. What did he want to
tell me? I've never met the feller.

RITA: That they've been established since 1912 and they've
had no complaints yet. [*Shrugs.*] Yiddishe business.

SYLVIA: Right. All done.

RITA: Really?

SYLVIA: Unless you suddenly decide you want to go blonde.
In which case I'd kill myself.

RITA: You're a marvel.

SYLVIA: My own worst enemy, believe me.

RITA: How much do I owe you, dear?

SYLVIA: It's my bar mitzvah present to Eliot.

RITA: You mustn't, Sylvia!

SYLVIA: It's my pleasure.

RITA: I wouldn't dream! Victor, did you hear what Sylvia
. . . we couldn't possibly . . .

VICTOR: I heard. I heard. [*To* SYLVIA] Thank you.

RITA [*calling*]: Eliot! Your dad and Lesley are waiting in the
car! If you . . .

[ELIOT *enters, wearing his new suit, and carrying a tallis
bag.*]

ELIOT: It was my cufflinks.

RITA: I left them out for you on the tallboy!

ELIOT: I couldn't do the right one with my left hand. It
wouldn't go. The shirt's stiff. The hole wouldn't open.

SYLVIA [*smiling at him, fondly*]: Well, you look beautiful . . .
A little mensch.

RITA [*to* ELIOT]: Well? Say thank you.

ELIOT: Thank you.

RITA: Right. Ready.
[*They all start moving round, collecting their accessories.*]
Coat. Handbag. [*To* SYLVIA, re *handbag*] Crocodile.
SYLVIA: Lovely.
RITA: Not *real*.
SYLVIA: No.
RITA [re *the handbag*]: Mail order. [*Resumes collecting her accessories.*] Gloves. Hat. Tallis bag! Victor – where's your tallis bag?
[VICTOR *holds it up for proof.*]
Eliot?
[*He holds up his tallis bag.*]
And your yarmulka?
ELIOT: Inside.
[*Throughout, while* RITA *is pivoting round,* SYLVIA *is trying to keep up with her, adding final touches to her hair.*]
LESLEY [*to* VICTOR]: Have I time to emigrate?
VICTOR: Another day. Tomorrow. I'll come with you. [*To* RITA] All ready, then? Have you taken a valium?
RITA: I've got. I've got. In my handbag. I've got.

38. Ext. House.

[VICTOR's *cab is parked outside.*
They all emerge from the front door.
RITA *sees the cab and stops, horrified, in her tracks.*]

RITA: We're not going in the cab?
VICTOR [*guiltily*]: What difference?
RITA: You said Richard Feldman was lending you his Escort!
VICTOR: He was. Now he says it's being serviced. You know what he's like.
RITA: Victor, for God's sake! It's his bar mitzvah!!
VICTOR [*making his way to the cab*]: For his wedding it'll be different . . .

RITA [*following unhappily*]: Thank you. I'll worry about that *next* week . . .

    [SYLVIA *follows* RITA, *giving little touches to her hair. The family embarks.*
    SYLVIA *stands waving goodbye as the cab drives off.*]

39. Ext. A street.

[*A man is hurrying down the street. He turns to see* VICTOR'S *cab driving along. He hails it.*]

40. Int. Cab. (Travelling.)

[VICTOR *is driving.*
LESLEY, RITA *and* ELIOT *are in their seats.*
VICTOR *sees the man and automatically touches his brakes.*]

RITA: Have you gone mad?
    [VICTOR *realizes his mistake, and accelerates again.*]
VICTOR: Habit. Force of habit. It can happen. [*He switches his meter on and continues on his way past the somewhat puzzled man who'd hailed him.*]

41. Int. Synagogue foyer.

[GRANDAD, *in his best clothes, is standing waiting. Other congregants enter and pass by, chatting to each other, meeting friends, wishing them good shabbos, shaking hands.*
At the main door, HAROLD *is keeping a lookout for the arrival of the family. He's dressed in his best clothes, and carries a camera case and various camera accessory cases.*
A WARDEN (*synagogue official*) *crosses to* GRANDAD.]

WARDEN: Mr Wax?

GRANDAD [*turning*]: Good shabbos!

WARDEN: Shabbos. Um ... your grandson's bar mitzvah this morning, am I right?

GRANDAD: Eliot. Yes. Eliot Green.

WARDEN: I've put you down to open the Ark, and his father to carry the scroll, all right?

GRANDAD [*deeply honoured*]: Thank you. A mitzvah. On behalf of his father and myself may I say ...

WARDEN: I'll give you the nod.

GRANDAD: Thank you.

[*The* WARDEN *continues busily on his way.*]

HAROLD [*turning from the door*]: O.K.

GRANDAD: They're here?

HAROLD: They're here.

[*He turns back to smile a welcome at* LESLEY, *as she enters with* VICTOR, RITA *and* ELIOT.

They exchange subdued greetings befitting the dignified surroundings they're now in.

GRANDAD *stands surveying* ELIOT *and* LESLEY *in happy pride.*]

GRANDAD: What can you say about perfection! Hadaigi – my cup brimmeth over.

RITA: How's your back?

GRANDAD: Who cares? Doctors also have to live. Listen, if the kids, bless them, are happy, you're happy. If you're happy, I'm happy. You're all happy, thank God, I'm the happiest man in the world. What should I do – cry?

42. Ext. Synagogue.

[*Over, u hear the normal Saturday morning service begin.*]

43. Int. Synagogue.

[*The service is in progress.* RABBI, *choir and congregants are singing.*

VICTOR, ELIOT, RITA, GRANDAD, LESLEY *and* HAROLD
are seated on the front row facing the RABBI *on his bimah.*

The men wear either yarmulka or hat (in VICTOR'*s case, a bowler)
and a tallis. The women also wear hats.* ELIOT *is wearing a brand-
new tallis and a white and gold yarmulka.*

VICTOR, RITA *and* GRANDAD *are now approaching a euphoric
climax of pride, anticipation, and tension. They turn, from time to
time, to exchange tense or sheepish smiles with friends in the congregation.*

HAROLD *is trying, as surreptitiously as possible, to slip a film
cassette into his camera.*

ELIOT *stares ahead, expressionlessly.*

The WARDEN *leaves the bimah (where he's been standing behind
the* RABBI*) and crosses the body of the synagogue towards the Ark,
where the holy scrolls are housed. On his way he almost imperceptibly
nods at* VICTOR *and* GRANDAD. *They at once get to their feet
and make their way – with somewhat uncharacteristic dignity –
towards the Ark. There,* GRANDAD *(briefly shown how by the*
WARDEN*) opens the richly-decorated curtains, and takes out the
heavy silver-ornamented scroll and hands it to* VICTOR. *The three
of them then return towards the bimah. En route,* GRANDAD
*reaches the seat he was sitting in before, and sits down again, his
duties now over. (A couple of people lean across to briefly shake his
hand.) The* WARDEN *and* VICTOR *continue to the bimah. They
mount it and join the* RABBI. VICTOR *places the scroll, with
extreme care, on to the* RABBI'*s lectern.*

(Throughout the above, intercut to RITA . . . *Now almost beside
herself with excitement; to* LESLEY, *proud almost in spite of herself; to* HAROLD, *struggling to fix a flash to his camera; and to*
ELIOT – *watching the bimah impassively.)*

The singing has now ended. The RABBI *opens the scroll and points
with a silver pointer to the relevant sentence.* VICTOR *takes the
fringed corner of his tallis, kisses it, then places it against the sentence in the scroll. He then raises the scroll, opened, with both hands
to slightly more than head height.*

At once the RABBI, *choir and congregation start to sing the following
in Hebrew:*]

'And it came to pass, when the Ark set forward, that Moses said Rise Up, O Lord, and thine enemies shall be scattered, and they that hate Thee shall flee before Thee. For out of Zion shall go forth the Law, and the word of the Lord from Jerusalem.'

[*During this,* VICTOR *turns to show the scroll to all sides of the synagogue.*]

RABBI [*in Hebrew*]: 'Blessed be he who in his holiness gave the law to his people Israel.'

[VICTOR *replaces the scroll on the lectern.*

A hush falls on the congregation: ELIOT's *moment has now arrived.*

Intercut between RITA, VICTOR, LESLEY, GRANDAD *and* HAROLD *(camera almost, almost ready).*]

RABBI [*calling out*]: Ya amod habarmitzvah Eliyahu bereb Velvel! 'Let the Bar mitzvah boy, Eliot son of Victor, now stand!'

[*He smiles encouragingly at* ELIOT.

ELIOT *stands and walks towards the bimah.*

RITA, VICTOR, GRANDAD, LESLEY *and* HAROLD *(through his viewfinder) watch him. Joy, love, pride and happiness cartwheeling along their veins with each thump of the heart.*

ELIOT *approaches the bimah, and with no change of pace, simply walks straight past it – and out of the door.*

A shock of absolute incomprehension thuds into everyone's face. Almost in slow motion. The shock gives way to disbelief, to confusion and to a rising babbling chaos. The service is disrupted. No one has the faintest idea what to do next.

VICTOR *stares at the* RABBI, *then at* RITA. *She stares back.*

HAROLD *lowers his camera.* VICTOR *stares back at the* RABBI. *The* RABBI *shrugs, dumbfounded. Everyone is at a total loss.*

VICTOR, *tentatively, after helpless glances at the* RABBI *and* RITA, *starts to leave the bimah, and half-run, half-walk to the door.*]

44. Ext. Synagogue.

ELIOT *emerges, stuffing his tallis and yarmulka into his pocket –
then suddenly starts racing like hell down the street and out of sight.
A moment or two later,* VICTOR, *the* WARDEN, WILFRED *the
caretaker and* HAROLD *appear at the door. They're followed a
moment or two later by* GRANDAD. *They look both ways.*
VICTOR *half-starts to run down the street, then stops, not knowing
which way to run.*
RITA *and* LESLEY *join them all at the door.
We hear the Saturday morning service falteringly resume.*]

45. Montage: Ext. Shopping streets.

[*Busy, bustling crowds of shoppers who've all got troubles of their
own.* ELIOT *meanders through them.
Over, we hear the synagogue service continuing.*]

46. Ext. Shopping street 'A'.

[*A small knot of men are standing looking at the merchandise in the
window of a girlie-magazine shop.
We pick up* ELIOT *walking down the street. He approaches the
magazine shop, but continues on his way into the shop next door.
This shop sells jokes and novelties. We stay on the shop façade.
After a moment,* ELIOT *reappears, now wearing a huge Mickey
Mouse mask which completely covers his face. He continues down the
street, feeling much more secure in his disguise.*]

47. Int. Café.

[*A teenagers' snackbar.
A few kids are sitting at tables. At a table on her own is* DENISE

(from Scene 1), sipping a Coke. Her swimming costume is in a rolled-up towel on the table.
ELIOT *enters, wearing his Mickey Mouse mask. On his way to the counter, he sees* DENISE.]

ELIOT: Hello.
　　　[*She looks up: A little scream, half-scared, half-amused.*]
DENISE: Who is it? ? ?
ELIOT: Me.
DENISE: I don't know who it is!
ELIOT: Me. C'est moi. Est ego.

48. Int. Synagogue foyer.

[*The service is now over. The last trickle of congregants is leaving, shaking hands with the* RABBI *and exchanging 'Good shabbos' wishes.*
The RABBI *turns and makes his way to his office.*]

49. Int. Rabbi's office.

[RITA, VICTOR, GRANDAD, LESLEY *and* HAROLD – *A tableau of white-faced shock, grief and bewilderment.*
WILFRED, *the caretaker, is handing cups of tea to them.*
RITA *is completely immobile in a chair.*
VICTOR *is shaking a little.* GRANDAD *is muttering to himself, helplessly, in Yiddish.*
HAROLD *is packing his camera equipment back in its cases.*
LESLEY *stares out of the window, deep in thought.*
The RABBI *enters.*
All dialogue in the scene is very subdued, spaced between long, heavy pauses and spoken almost in the dead whispers of a bereavement.]

RABBI: Um . . . well . . . good shabbos.
HAROLD: Good shabbos.
　　　[*The others ignore him.*]

RABBI [*to* WILFRED]: Have *you* had a cup?

WILFRED: It's sweet tea. Very sweet. For medicinal purposes. I didn't think you'd want any.

RABBI: I didn't. No . . .

[WILFRED *exits.*

The RABBI *flops down in his chair behind his desk.*]

[*Helplessly*] Well now.

[*A very long silence.*]

LESLEY: What happens in cases like this?

RABBI: There are no cases like this.

LESLEY: No.

RABBI: There's no such thing.

[*A long silence.*]

HAROLD [*to* LESLEY]: Would you like a valium?

LESLEY: In my mum's handbag.

HAROLD: And would you *like* one?

VICTOR: There's none left.

50. Int. Café.

[*The Mickey Mouse mask is lying on the table.*

ELIOT *is now seated opposite* DENISE, *both drinking Cokes.*]

ELIOT: Didn't Squidge go swimming?

DENISE: He left early. He banged his toes on the side of the bath. He went home crying.

ELIOT: 'Crying'? ? ?

DENISE: Well, he banged his toe, didn't he!

ELIOT [*puzzled*]: He's over thirteen, though, is Squidge.

[*A pause.*]

ELIOT: I've run away.

DENISE: From home?

ELIOT: No. Just away.

DENISE: Why?

[*A pause.*]

ELIOT: Where are you going now?

DENISE: Home. It's mince cutlets. I hate mince cutlets. I'm a vegetarian but they won't believe me. I've been vegetarian for over a fortnight.

ELIOT: Do you fancy a picnic instead? An open-air picnic?

DENISE: *I* know! In Jackson Street playground!

ELIOT: O.K. [*He gets up.*] See you there in half an hour. I've this mission to accomplish first. [*He exits.*]

51. Int. Rita's kitchen.

[HAROLD *is making worsht sandwiches.*
GRANDAD *is seated at the table.*
LESLEY *is serving him with a bowl of soup.*
GRANDAD *is dismissing the offer of soup.*]

GRANDAD: I've no appetite.

LESLEY: Of course you have.
    [*He shakes his head.*]
It'll give you one.

GRANDAD: How can anyone eat with a broken heart?

LESLEY: Practice makes perfect. [*Relenting*] Sorry.
    [GRANDAD *begins, very gently, to cry.*]

LESLEY: Ssshhh, now. Sssshhh. Try a little soup.

GRANDAD: Lesley?

LESLEY: Mmm?

HAROLD [re *the sandwiches he's making*]: Tomato sauce or brown sauce?
    [*They ignore him.*]   On the worsht?
    [*They ignore him.*]

GRANDAD [*to* LESLEY]: I'd been looking forward.

LESLEY: Yes, I know. We all had.

GRANDAD: I'd bought him a watch for his bar mitzvah present. [*He takes it out of his pocket.*] *Shock*proof, eppas!

HAROLD [re *the sandwiches*]: Or mustard?

VICTOR [*O.O.V. in living room, calling urgently*]: Lesley!!

LESLEY: What?

52. Int. Living room.

[VICTOR *is standing at the telephone dialling a number.*]

VICTOR [*yelling towards the kitchen*]: What did you say his name was?

LESLEY [*O.O.V.*]: Squidge. Eliot calls him Squidge.

VICTOR: Squidge *what*, for Christ's sake! I mean if his father answers – I've never met the feller – how can I –

LESLEY [*O.O.V.*]: Squidge Pearlman.

VICTOR: And is Squidge his real – [*Then suddenly into phone*] Oh . . . um . . . good afternoon! Mrs Pearlman? . . . I'm er . . . I'm sorry to trouble you . . . is Eliot Green there, please? Squidge's pal. [*Pause.*] Sorry, you believe what? [*Pause.*] I see. Thank you.
    [*He replaces the receiver.*
    LESLEY *pops her head in from kitchen.*]

LESLEY: No?

VICTOR: No. She believes it's his bar mitzvah today. [*Sighs*] Punkt! [*Pause.*] Well, now? Who else? [*A pause. He's almost in tears, through anger, incomprehension and hurt.*] Lesley, I'll murder him. I will. I've spent thirteen years bringing him up; and now I've done it, I'll bloody strangle him!

HAROLD [*O.O.V.*]: Lesley? Would your mother prefer tomato sauce, brown sauce or mustard? Or none of them?
    [*They ignore him.*]

VICTOR: Doesn't he pal out with Maurice Donner's lad – whatsisname?

LESLEY: Stewart.

VICTOR: Stewart. Where's he live? What's his number?

LESLEY: Dad. They haven't palled out since they were six! Seeing who could wee the highest.

HAROLD [*entering from the kitchen*]: Scuse me, man at work. [*He squeezes past them, carrying a tray on which there's a bowl of soup and sandwiches. He exits to the stairs.*]

53. Ext. 'Solly the Barber's'.

[*A 'closed' sign is hanging in the glass door.*
ELIOT *approaches, wearing his mask. He tries the handle. Peers through the door. Knocks.*
SOLLY *opens the door. Sees* **ELIOT** *in his mask.*]

SOLLY: Oy a-clog!!
ELIOT: Can I have a haircut, please?
SOLLY [*indicating the 'closed' sign*]: Cuck! Closed.
ELIOT: I've come for one because I want to. Not because everybody else wants me to. I *don't* come when everybody else wants me to. It's a rule.
SOLLY: When it says closed, I'm closed. That's another rule. Saturday's the Jewish Sunday, pal. Shabbos. Day of prayer.
　　[*He closes the door.*
　　Immediate cut to:]

54. Int. 'Solly the Barber's'.

[*Solly turns from closing the door and starts to make his way back into the shop – where three men seated in barber's chairs are playing cards on a table in the middle.*]

SOLLY: Now, where was I? Oh, yes. See you for 20p, Moishe.
MOISHE: Three tens, pair of Queens.
SOLLY: Me and my big mouth.

55. Int. Parents' bedroom.

[**RITA** *is lying on the bed facing the ceiling. She's wearing her dressing gown. Her bar mitzvah dress is hanging on a hanger outside the wardrobe. She's been crying.*

HAROLD *is seated by the bed, holding the tray of food.*]

HAROLD [*a pause*]: A mouthful. Try one mouthful.

RITA [*without looking*]: No, thank you, Harold.

HAROLD: It's bean and barley. Your favourite. You cooked it.

[*A pause.* RITA *lies staring up at the ceiling. Her eyes fill up again.*]

HAROLD [*lamely*]: And a worsht sandwich.

RITA [*calling*]: Victor?

VICTOR [*O.O.V., calling*]: I'm on the phone!

RITA [*calling*]: Victor, come here.

[HAROLD *puts the tray down and sits beside the bed. He sighs, helplessly.*]

HAROLD: I mean you just don't know what to suggest, do you? It's never been heard of. Your bar mitzvah, it's something you . . . [*he gestures ineffectually*] All the months of . . . All the expense. Who's heard of a Jewish boy not getting bar mitzvah'd? It's something you don't *hear* of. I mean you're his mother – you could have a heart attack. You could lie there and have a heart attack! I mean Mr *Wax* isn't a young man . . .

[VICTOR *hurries in.*]

VICTOR [*concerned, quietly urgent*]: Has she started sweating again? [*To* RITA] Are your legs shaking?

[RITA *stares into the middle-distance. Extremely distraught, almost literally ill, she speaks with an ominous calmness – very slowly.*]

RITA: Victor. At this moment . . . on their way . . . are 117 guests. At this moment. They're sitting on the train. In cars. Queuing for buses. All on their way. At half past six, Victor, 117 people from Bournemouth, from Manchester, Leeds and Glasgow, from Birmingham, everywhere, are going to turn up at the Reuben Shulman Hall expecting a dinner-dance. All dressed up. Your uncle Zalman. My cousin Freda. Your brother we don't talk about from Cardiff.

VICTOR: Sssshhh. Don't upset yourself.

RITA [*oblivious to him*]: 117 people. 117 portions of chopped liver. 117 mushroom vol-au-vents. 117 chicken with croquette potatoes and helzel, French beans and cole slaw. 117 lokshen cuggles, a three-piece band – and no bar mitzvah boy. No bar mitzvah. No nothing.

VICTOR: It's no help upsetting yourself.

RITA [*oblivious to him*]: So, tell me, how do we cancel? How do we stop trains and cars and tell everyone to go home again? Do we stand on the M.1 with a notice-board? Do we stand outside the Reuben Shulman Hall and tell them Eliot's gone for a walk and they've got no dinner? Ring Levy's and tell them we accidentally made a mistake – it was *next* year? What do we say? Do *we* go? Do *we* turn up? Do we ever show our face *again*? You're a clever man, you read the newspapers, you argue politics, tell me. I'd like to know.

> [*A helpless silence.*
> RITA*'s eyes start to fill up again.*
> VICTOR *and* HAROLD *stare uselessly down at their shoes.*]

HAROLD: Shall I ring the police again?

> [*They ignore him. A silence.*]

RITA: 117 guests. All in their evening suits. Long dresses. Sequin handbags.

> [*A pause.*]

VICTOR [*quietly, calmly, matter-of-fact*]: They *say* they break your heart. It's an old saying. My *father* said it. 'Children break your heart.' [*Pause.*] I'll break every bone in his body.

56. Ext. Children's playground.

[ELIOT *and* DENISE *are at one edge of the playground, on a bench or sitting on the grass, picknicking on sweets and toffees.*
Some distance away, gangs of kids are playing, fighting, laughing or crying.]

ELIOT: I'd been learning them for nearly a year. All the prayers etcetera. Today the supposed intention was to stand up in the synagogue and say them.

DENISE: Why didn't you then?

ELIOT: It's the day that marks my passage from boyhood to manhood.

DENISE: Oh, is *that* the passage? [*Disappointed.*] Oh, I see . . .

ELIOT: Once you've said the prayers etcetera, you're a grown man. That's the supposed intention.

[*A pause.* DENISE *selects another sweet.*]

DENISE: Are you scared what'll happen?

ELIOT: No. A bit.

DENISE: Because of Jesus?

ELIOT: Jesus Christ?

DENISE: Yes.

ELIOT: No – because of my mum and dad. They're anxious parents. They've probably committed suicide by now. Perished by human hand.

[*A pause.*]

DENISE: The day my mum took me to get my first bra, that night, well, I cried all night in bed. [*Pause.*] It's nothing – standing up saying prayers. Christian girls have a worse day than that before they're grown up.

[ELIOT *isn't listening.*]

I said Christian girls have an even worse day. Of an intimate nature. I'll probably never get over it, personally. It comes as this sudden shock but you haven't to be frightened. Anyway, then you're a woman. Official. I'm going now. [*She's on her feet immediately.*]

ELIOT: Now???

DENISE: You get on my nerves, actually. Does Squidge know you're here?

ELIOT: No one does.

DENISE: Is it a secret?

ELIOT: Well, obviously.

DENISE: Is there only me that knows?

ELIOT: It was you that *suggested* it when *I* said picnic! !
  [*A tiny pause.*]
DENISE: I'm quite good at secrets.

57. Int. Hallway.

[VICTOR *is admitting* RABBI SHERMAN *into the house.*]

VICTOR [*worriedly*]: Thank you, Rabbi.
RABBI: Listen. [*Meaning ' It's the least I could do.'*]
VICTOR: Very good of you.
  [*The* RABBI *pats him sympathetically on the shoulder.*]
RABBI: Upstairs?
  [VICTOR *nods and indicates the way. They start up the stairs.
  Cut to* GRANDAD, *at the living room door, watching them.*]
GRANDAD [*to* HAROLD *in the living room*]: The rabbi's here.
HAROLD [*O.O.V.*]: Yes.
GRANDAD [*worriedly*]: She's that bad?
HAROLD [*O.O.V.*]: He *wanted* to come.
GRANDAD [*brightening*]: He'll make everything all right,
  maybe.
HAROLD [*O.O.V.*]: How?
  [GRANDAD *has no answer. The question makes him feel even
  more helpless.*]

58. Int. Parents' bedroom.

[RITA *is now in bed.*
LESLEY *is sitting on the side of the bed.*]

RITA: I never did like that wallpaper. It was all the rage
  when we put it up. I've gone cold again.
LESLEY: Shall I make you a hot-water bottle?
RITA: And the next minute I'm schwitzing. You look pale,
  Lesley.

LESLEY: I'm a bit tired, that's all.

RITA: You're paler than any of us. Would you like to borrow some of my Blush and Gloss?

LESLEY: No, thanks.

RITA [*ignoring the reply*]: In my handbag. On the dressing table.

[*We hear footsteps climbing the stairs during the above.*]

VICTOR [*O.O.V.*]: There we are.

RABBI: Thank you.

[VICTOR *and the* RABBI *enter.*

LESLEY *smiles briefly at the* RABBI. *He shrugs philosophically in reply.*

RITA'*s eyes immediately start to brim over again.*

The RABBI *sits on the edge of the bed.*

VICTOR *hovers awkwardly around.*]

[*Sighing*] Well now.

[*Another helpless silence. No one has anything to say.*]

No news from the police, I imagine?

VICTOR: Police. What can you do? The sergeant didn't seem to think it was all that serious.

RABBI [*brief smile*]: Not a Yiddishe sergeant – am I wrong?

[VICTOR *smiles briefly in response to the joke.*

A silence.]

LESLEY [*to* RABBI]: I'll make you a cup of tea.

[*He smiles his thanks, sadly.*

LESLEY *exits.*]

59. Int. Phone kiosk.

[DENISE *enters. She selects the 'E to K' directory and starts looking for a number.*]

60. Int. Living room.

[LESLEY *is crossing from the kitchen, carrying a cup of tea.*
GRANDAD *is in an easy chair gazing at the watch he'd bought for*
ELIOT. *He sees* LESLEY *with the cup.*]

GRANDAD: No, thank you, darling. I'll make if I want.
LESLEY: It's not for you. It's for Rabbi Sherman.
[*The phone rings abruptly.*
LESLEY *puts the cup and saucer down and lifts the receiver*
urgently.]
[*Into phone*] Hello?

61. Int. Phone kiosk.

[DENISE *is speaking into the phone.*]

DENISE: Is that Eliot's mother?
[*Intercut between* DENISE *and* LESLEY *as required.*]
LESLEY: His sister. Who's that?
DENISE: If you're looking for Eliot, he is in Jackson Street
Playground. He is perfectly sound in wind and limb.
This is someone he split on at school yesterday who prefers
to remain anonymous. Yours sincerely, A Well-wisher.
[*She replaces the phone.*]

62. Int. Living room.

[LESLEY *slams the phone down and races into the hallway.*
GRANDAD *watches, puzzled by her haste.*]

63. Int. Hallway.

[LESLEY *races from the living room, and grabs her coat from the hallstand.*
HAROLD *emerges with the untouched tray from the parents' bedroom. He sees* LESLEY.]

HAROLD: Are you going out?
LESLEY: Shan't be long.
HAROLD: Where are you going? Shall *I* go for you?
    [LESLEY *dashes out and slams the door behind her.*]

64. Int. Parents' bedroom.

[RITA *is in bed.*
The RABBI *is sitting on the bed.*
VICTOR *is sitting in a chair.*]

RITA: What's happening?
HAROLD [*re-entering*]: She's popped out a minute. Don't know where. I'd have gone for her if she'd have wanted. I offered.
VICTOR [*half to himself*]: First him. Now her. Like the exodus from bloody Egypt. [*To the* RABBI] No disrespect.

65. Int. Living room.

[GRANDAD *gets up from his easy chair, sighing philosophically.*]

GRANDAD: Aye, aye, aye, aye, aye ... Life. [*Unthinkingly he picks up the* RABBI's *cup of tea and wanders back to his chair.*] You try ... You do your best ... It's not easy ... Listen, if it was *easy* ... and that's ... er ... always has been, always will be ... and ... er ... [*His rambling*

66

peters away into a vague shrug that's somehow supposed to conclude his argument. He settles down in his chair and starts drinking from the cup.]

66. Ext. Children's playground.

[ELIOT *is still sitting in the same place, watching the group of kids playing.*
LESLEY *enters the playground.* ELIOT *spots her peering round searching for him and immediately puts on his Mickey Mouse mask.*
LESLEY *sees him, and immediately knows it's him. She strolls unhurriedly over to him and sits beside him.*
A pause. They both sit watching the children.]

LESLEY: I should always wear it. It's a hell of an improvement.
   [*He at once takes it off.*
   They sit watching the children.]
Having a terrific time, are you? We've had a terrific time. We went to the synagogue. It was a good laugh. Pity you couldn't stay.
   [ELIOT *seems to have decided never to speak again. He sits watching the children.*]
Listen, Nutcase. There are two alternatives. Either we talk, or I smash your face in. It's entirely up to you. [*No reply.*] In a minute, there'll be *one* alternative.

ELIOT: Are they upset?

LESLEY: 'Upset'?

ELIOT: Are they?

LESLEY: Oh, brilliant! No, they're having bloody singsong! Eliot – for God's sake – the most important day of their lives!
   [*A pause.*]
Well?
   [ELIOT *shrugs. Then sighs.*]

ELIOT: I went for a haircut by the way.

LESLEY: You what??

ELIOT: I didn't have one though.

LESLEY: You went for a *bar mitzvah* . . . you didn't have one of those either! What the hell do you mean you went for a haircut! Is that why you left? To go for a sodding haircut?

ELIOT: 'Course not.

LESLEY: Well, why?

[*A pause.*

Why, Eliot?

ELIOT: I don't think I'm old enough to be bar mitzvah'd.

[LESLEY *stares at him, completely nonplussed.*]

LESLEY: You're thirteen. That's the *age.*

ELIOT: I don't think I've got the qualifications.

LESLEY: *What* qualifications? The only qualification is to be thirteen! All you've to do is breathe for thirteen years and avoid the *traffic*! What the hell are you talking about?

[*A pause.*

A ball rolls towards them, accidentally thrown there by a couple of kids playing. ELIOT *picks it up and throws it back to them.*]

ELIOT: I don't think I believe in them, Lesley.

LESLEY: In what?

ELIOT: Bar mitzvahs. I don't think they work.

LESLEY [*confused, exasperated*]: Eliot. Every Jewish boy gets bar mitzvah'd. Every single one. For thousands of years!

ELIOT [*helpfully*]: Five thousand seven hundred and thirty six.

LESLEY [*accepting his help*]: Five thousand seven hundred and thirty six. Everybody. Dad did it. Grandad. Harold . .

ELIOT: They're not men, Lesley.

[*The simple sentence is like a terrible smack across the face. Calm now, very grave, very concerned,* LESLEY *stares at him.*]

That's the whole point. If that's being a man, I don't want to be one, do I? And it was no good pretending I did.

[*A pause.*

68

LESLEY *is beginning to understand the truth of what he's said. It hurts her and saddens her.*]

LESLEY [*lamely*]: What are they then? If they're not men? Giraffes?

[*A pause.*

The ball comes rolling towards them again from the two children playing. They're both too preoccupied to return it.]

FIRST KID [*calling*]: Can we have our ball back, missus? [*Pause.*] Oy! Grandma! Cloth-ears!

[LESLEY, *absently, throws it back to them.*]

LESLEY [*apprehensive about what* ELIOT *may reply*]: Dad's a man, Eliot . . .

ELIOT [*calmly, reasonably; he's thought it all out many times before*]: If he was my age and behaved like he does, he'd get a clip round the ear. Dad's a big spoilt kid, Lesley. Do you know why I wouldn't go for a haircut yesterday? Because everybody wanted me to. I was being a stupid kid. Awkward. Like dad. He doesn't care tuppence what other people want. That's ignorant, really, in a grown man.

[*A pause.*]

LESLEY [*even more apprehensively*]: And Harold?

ELIOT: Harold does everything that everybody wants. That's even worse. He's scared *not* to. He's scared all the time. *You* ought to know. [*Pause.*] Grandad wants everybody to think the world of him just because he's Grandad. Just because he's there. Like babies do. Little babies in prams.

[*A pause.*

LESLEY *knows it's all true. The more certain she is, the angrier she feels towards* ELIOT: *she wants to lash out wildly.*]

LESLEY: And that's what you think, is it?

ELIOT [*sadly*]: Rotten, isn't it? It makes my chest hurt.

LESLEY: It's your considered opinion?

ELIOT: I'm not saying they're the only ones. That's the trouble. It's every feller you . . .

LESLEY: Well, here's *my* considered opinion, Eliot. You're a bloody liar! It's all an excuse, you lying sod! You ran away because you couldn't do it! Because you were frightened you'd forgotten what you'd learnt!

ELIOT: I wasn't, Lesley.

LESLEY: You thought you'd get it all wrong! That you'd make a nudnik of yourself! You were chicken!

ELIOT [*wearily*]: Lesley, I could do it standing on my head.

LESLEY: Go on, then! Prove it!

ELIOT: Look, all I'm saying is . . .

LESLEY: I know what you're saying! That all the men you've ever known . . . and your own dad, and Grandad, and Harold . . . all did what you couldn't! What you weren't even man enough to *try*!

ELIOT: They did . . . but they *didn't* . . . [*With growing frustration*] . . . they didn't mean what they . . .

LESLEY: They *tried*! They're *still* bloody trying for all you know! *You* didn't! And they're the babies? You're a liar, Eliot. The whole thing's an excuse. You're a bloody liar.
    [*A pause.*]

ELIOT [*almost to himself*]: I could do it standing on my head . . .
    [*A pause.*
    LESLEY *watches the kids playing, then, as though she considers the discussion over, she gets up and starts brushing grass from her clothes, apparently ready to leave.*
    ELIOT *sits staring ahead at the children playing. After a moment or two, he gets to his feet, puts his hands on the ground and levers himself up so that he's standing on his head. He begins to recite the first Hebrew blessing of his bar mitzvah.*
    LESLEY *stares at him, blankly.*]

67. Int. Parents' Bedroom.

[RITA *is in bed.*
The RABBI *sits on the edge of the bed.*

VICTOR *wheels round angrily, in the middle of a row with* RITA.]

VICTOR: Why me? Why pick on me? What do you mean
'I'm a great help, I always have been'?

RITA: You're his father.

VICTOR: So what am I supposed to do!

RITA [*wearily*]: I can't argue. I'm sick of arguing.

VICTOR: I do my bloody share, Rita!

RITA: Share of shouting, yes! That, you're good at. The
big man. The ganzy macher. Shouting and bawling!
But never *doing*! Never since I've known you!

VICTOR: Doing what?

RITA: Anything!

VICTOR: I go and play every day, don't I? Twiddling my
thumbs. The rent pays itself. Clothes. Food. I don't know
what else I'm supposed to do, for crying out loud!

RITA [*sighing*]: I know you don't.

68. Ext. Children's playground.

[ELIOT *and* LESLEY.
ELIOT *is still standing on his head, reaching the end of his recita-
tion of his portion of the law.*
LESLEY *is watching.*]

ELIOT: Can I do it the right way up now?

[LESLEY *shrugs.* ELIOT *rolls over into a sitting position and
continues with the blessing after the reading of the scroll.*]

69. Int. Kitchen.

[GRANDAD *is asleep in a chair.*
We hear, indistinctly but loudly, the shouting match between RITA
and VICTOR *increasing in violence O.O.V. Suddenly we hear a
smash.*

GRANDAD *jerks awake.*]

GRANDAD [*at once; absolutely automatically*]: Mazeltov! Listen, if they're happy, you're happy. If you're happy, thank God, I'm happy. It's my happiness – a wonderful family. What should I do . . . cry?

70. Ext. Children's playground.

[ELIOT *and* LESLEY.
ELIOT *is reciting his portion from the Bible.*]

71. Int. Living room.

[VICTOR, HAROLD, *and the* RABBI *are sitting in silence.*
RITA *enters in her dressing gown and sits down. The row has ended.* RITA *and* VICTOR *are still quietly simmering.
The* RABBI *is embarrassed,* HAROLD *glum.*]

RITA: Harold, am I right or am I wrong?
HAROLD [*scared at suddenly being involved*]: What?
RITA: Who's right?
VICTOR: What's it got to do with him?
HAROLD: Nothing.
VICTOR: Sticking his bloody oar in . . .
RITA: Harold?
HAROLD [*wriggling*]: Um . . . well, well, actually, it's not really for me to say . . . um . . .
RITA: It is if I ask you. You have my permission.
VICTOR: And mine. Go on: Who's right?
    [*They both look at* HAROLD. *He looks from one to the other. petrified of offending either.*]
HAROLD: Well, in some respects, there seems to be some truth in what . . .
VICTOR: Which respects?

72

HAROLD [*hastily*]: Not *all*. I didn't say *all*.

RITA: Which?

> [HAROLD *sits speechless with fear.*
> *A pause.*]

VICTOR: Well, *speak*! For once in your life, *upset* someone!

HAROLD: Um ... well, actually, in many respects, you're *both* right. I think there's a lot to be said for ... um ... for what you both said. I agree with you both. [*A beat.*] Wholeheartedly.

72. Ext. Children's playground.

> [ELIOT *and* LESLEY.
> ELIOT *is coming to the end of the last of the Hebrew blessings.*]

ELIOT: Amen. [*He looks at* LESLEY.] I said 'Amen'.

LESLEY [*subdued*]: Amen.

> [*A pause.*]

ELIOT: Told you I could do it.

LESLEY [*sighing*]: Yes. Mazeltov. [*She looks at him.*] I said 'Mazeltov'.

ELIOT: Thanks. [*He offers* LESLEY *the bag of sweets.*] Want to take a bit of enamel off your teeth?

> [*She shakes her head.*]

I'd have said it even better with the scroll in front of me. You're not expected to know it by heart. [*Pause.*] I was good, wasn't I?

LESLEY: *I* don't know. It's all Chinese to me.

ELIOT: Mmm, I was. I was pretty good.

LESLEY: Shame, then, isn't it?

ELIOT: What is?

LESLEY: You could've been the first. The first man. Seeing there are no others. The first man since Adam. [*She looks at* ELIOT. Do you reckon *he* was O.K.?

ELIOT: I've never met the feller.

LESLEY: That would've suited you, wouldn't it?

ELIOT [*yes, it would*]: He wasn't bar mitzvah'd at *all*. He had no religion.

LESLEY: The first ever then. In the history of Man.

ELIOT [*haltingly, thoughtfully*]: It's all right *saying* it. It's *keeping* it. I mean, the ten commandments must be a pig to *start* with. [*Pause.*] They've all *said* it. They probably all meant it. At the time, anyway. At their bar mitzvah. I mean that's hard, but I expect it gets even harder. [*Pause.*] It probably gets harder and harder as you go on. There's the rub.

LESLEY: I think what *you* did was the hardest of all.

[ELIOT *looks at her, puzzled.*]

Not getting bar mitzvah'd.

ELIOT: That was easy!

LESLEY: Only to you. [*Pause.*] You know a lot more about it than I do ... but I think it was probably the most grown-up thing I've ever heard of.

[*A pause.*]

ELIOT: That wasn't the intended intention.

LESLEY: I know it wasn't. [*She smiles.*] Hard luck.

ELIOT [*thoughtfully*]: Do you think I'm probably a man already then?

LESLEY: I think you're on your way.

ELIOT: Whether I want to or not?

LESLEY: In your case.

ELIOT [*subdued*]: Wow. [*Pause.*] It's a bit bloody scary.

LESLEY: Why do you think they all make such a tsimmes of it? And there's no need to swear!

[*Pause.*]

ELIOT: I think I feel a bit sick now.

LESLEY: Come home, join the club.

ELIOT: And would that be grown up ... going home again?

LESLEY: Very.

ELIOT: I expect I'll have to tell a few lies, won't I?

LESLEY: I'll tell the lies. I've had the practice. I've been grown-up for years.

[ELIOT *sits for a moment, then slowly gets up.*

They gather up their belongings and start to walk away to the exit of the playground. The Mickey Mouse mask is left lying on the grass.]

73. Int. Living room.

[RITA *is wrapped in her dressing gown.*
VICTOR, HAROLD *and* GRANDAD *sit facing* LESLEY *and* ELIOT.
The RABBI *sits to one side.*]

LESLEY [*quietly*]: He was worried.

VICTOR [*yelling*]: *He* was worried???!! [*To* ELIOT] *You* were bloody worried???!!

RITA: Worried about your mother dying of a broken heart? Thank you. Chutzpa! You broke it!

HAROLD: People *here* were worried, my lad, did you know that? I mean your poor mother . . . your grandfather . . .

VICTOR [*interrupting violently*]: You do arithmetic at school, do you? Do you know how much the Reuben Shulman Hall costs at £7.50 a head, 117 heads!?

LESLEY [*finding the words with difficulty*]: He had his reasons. He *thought* he had his reasons. He's only a kid. He's *not* actually. He was worried, that's all.

RABBI: Worried you couldn't remember what you'd learnt, Eliot? The Hebrew?

LESLEY: Not that. He knows that backwards. [*A tiny smile at* ELIOT.] Well . . . upside down. [*To the* RABBI] He did it.

RABBI [*puzzled*]: Did what?

LESLEY: The lot. Word for word.

[*They all stare at her, dumbfounded.*]

RITA: What do you mean he did it? He walked out! I was *there*! With a fifteen guinea hat on, kvelling!

LESLEY: He did it for me. In the kid's playground.

[*A silence. They all look at* ELIOT, *then back at* LESLEY.]

RABBI: He recited his bar mitzvah? ? By heart? ?

ELIOT: Word perfect.

VICTOR [*to* ELIOT]: God, you really do put the boot in, don't you, mate! [*to the* RABBI] Next time you've got a bar mitzvah, move the shul to the kids' playground! Ring MacAlpines'! Get an estimate!

GRANDAD [*gently*]: So what were you worried about, Tattele? Tell me.

[LESLEY *and* ELIOT *exchange a glance.* LESLEY *looks thoughtfully from* VICTOR, *to* GRANDAD, *to* HAROLD.]

LESLEY: He thought . . . He thought he couldn't be the man . . . well, the sort of man you'd expect him to be . . . A man like *you*. And Dad. And Harold.

[*A silence. All touched by* LESLEY's *words.*

VICTOR *goes over to* ELIOT *and sits on his haunches in front of him. He takes* ELIOT's *hands in his.*]

VICTOR [*tenderly, expansively*]: Eliot. Barm-pot. To you I seem like a God . . . a hero. It's only natural. Natural but stupid. We're not all that wonderful. We've all got faults. *Little* ones, maybe. But we've got them. Sometimes I've been a bit of a lobbos. When I was younger perhaps. I wasn't all that perfect. Nor Zaidy here . . .

GRANDAD: 'Course not . . .

VICTOR: A fine man. But not every second of the day! And Harold. A fine boy. A gutanashomma, certainly. But sometimes – not often – a bit of a shlemiel.

HAROLD: Now and then.

VICTOR: We've *all* got little faults. You just haven't noticed them, that's all. Only because we've learnt to hide them. In the fullness of time.

RABBI [*very, very thoughtfully, very quietly*]: Mr Green, Mrs Green . . . there's a prayer we say in shul. A prayer for mourners . . .

RITA: No one's died! Who's died?

RABBI: For *all* of us one day. It begins 'Hamacoum yena-chaim etchem . . .'

VICTOR [*totally none-the-wiser*]: Oh, yes?

RABBI: It means 'May the Almighty comfort you'.

GRANDAD [*to himself*]: Amen.

VICTOR [*to* RABBI]: Oh, yes?

RABBI: Now [*carefully, working out his train of thought as he goes*] the point is . . . Hamacoum means 'place', meaning *every* place, meaning everywhere, meaning God. God means anywhere, everywhere. A synagogue, a bedroom, a battlefield, a playground. [*Turns to* ELIOT.] You did the full portion, Eliot?

ELIOT: Yes.

RABBI: Everything?

ELIOT: I got stuck on 'machpailah' in the bit about Esther and the cave, but I went back and got it right.

[*A very pregnant pause. Everyone looks at the* RABBI.]

RABBI: Now the thing is . . . Mr Green, are there any jobs going on your taxi-tank?

VICTOR: Eh?

RABBI: By Monday morning I may need one. Car-washing would be a nice change. I'll bring my own wash-leather.

VICTOR: Eh?

RABBI: For what I'm going to say, I may get a few nasty memos from high up. From *fairly* high up. But not from as high up as God, I don't think.

[*He shrugs, smiles a little worriedly at them all.
A pause.*]

VICTOR [*irritated*]: And what *are* you going to say?

RABBI: What I'm going to say is that, in my view – Eliot is now bar mitzvah.

[*A shocked silence.*]

RITA: Pardon?

RABBI: If he did it, he did it.

VICTOR: In Jackson Street playground? ? ?

RABBI: 'Hamacoum' – anywhere. [*He gets up, goes over to* ELIOT *and shakes his hand.*] Mazeltov. You're a man, young man. How's it feel?

[*A brief pause while* ELIOT *considers.*]

ELIOT: Not much different, really. Bit more tired, that's all.

74. Int. Banqueting hall. Evening.

[*Open on the* MASTER OF CEREMONIES, *stationed at the door to the foyer. He calls, above the babbling conversation of the 117 guests, clearly and imperiously.*]

MASTER OF CEREMONIES: Pray be upstanding to receive your host and hostess – and Bar Mitzvah Boy!
  [*We now see the hall populated with the evening-dressed guests, all rising to their feet from their numbered dining tables.*
  At the head table, GRANDAD, LESLEY *and* HAROLD (*struggling to fix his flash to his camera*) *all rise proudly.*
  The three-piece band strikes up with 'Sholem Aleichem', with the entire assembly clapping in rhythm and singing the words.
  ELIOT, *followed by* VICTOR *and* RITA, *enters from the foyer and walks towards his place of honour at the head table* (*his seat will be between* VICTOR *and* RITA).
  The music, singing and clapping continues until ELIOT *has reached his seat and sat down.*
  Everyone else sits.]
VICTOR [*to* RITA]: Thank God for that!
RITA: For what?
VICTOR: For one terrible minute I thought he was going to walk straight past the bloody table, and out of the bloody window . . .

75. Int. Hall.

[*The assembled guests are tucking into their chopped liver, amid a deafening babble of conversation. We see a few shrugged shoulders at the quality of the chopped liver; a few guests waving to friends at other tables, or leaning over their neighbours, rudely, to shake hands; and a few disapproving glances on studying the rest of the menu.*]

76. Int. Hall.

[VICTOR *eating his mushroom vol-au-vent with the appetite of a reprieved convict.*]

RITA: Victor?
VICTOR: I'm busy.
RITA: If any of them were there this morning . . . when Eliot
    . . . When Eliot didn't – they'll know he never – I mean
    what shall we say happened?
VICTOR: *You're* a ligner. You'll think of something.
RITA: What, though?
VICTOR: Rita, do me a favour. *Worry* about it.

77. Int. Hall.

[GRANDAD, *now eating the main course, turns to watch* HAROLD *who is struggling perplexedly with his camera.*]

GRANDAD: It's a wonderful thing, a camera. All the pic-
    tures . . . everybody happy. You look at them. You
    remember. It's a wonderful thing!
HAROLD [*calmly hysterical*]: All double exposures. Every one
    of them. Double exposure. Every single one.

78. Int. Hall.

[LESLEY *is about to start eating her lockshen pudding. She leans
backwards to reach round* VICTOR *and taps* ELIOT *on the shoulder.*]

LESLEY: Hey, do you want my lockshen cuggle?
ELIOT: Don't you?

LESLEY: It's fattening. Anyway, I can't eat properly, I've got a cold sore. Give us your plate.

ELIOT: Is it allowed?

LESLEY: Why not?

ELIOT: Well . . . etiquette, etcetera.

LESLEY: No such thing.

ELIOT: It's only ritual, really, isn't it? Load of rubbish, really, isn't it – ritual?

LESLEY: That's all.

ELIOT: That's all. C'est tout. Est omnium.

79. Int. Hall.

[*A waitress is going from guest to guest asking 'Russian tea or black coffee?' and pouring from jugs. She goes along the head table, and inadvertently overlooks asking the* RABBI.

RABBI [*holding up his cup as she wanders by*]: Miss! Miss! Excuse me, Miss!
    [*She doesn't hear.*]

80. Int. Hall.

[*The meal is over.* RITA *sits back and sighs, contentedly.*]

RITA: Victor?

VICTOR [*lighting an uncustomary cigar*]: Again she's here with her 'Victor' . . .!

RITA: Can you tell me why I worry about them? The kids? Twenty years from now, they'll still be going their own sweet way, happy, unhappy, what difference? – and I'll have worried myself into the grave. 'Twenty' years – what am I talking about? *Five* years. Six *months. Any* time. Perhaps I should ask when it'd be convenient for *them.* Next Tuesday, maybe. I'll leave Wednesday's dinner on a low light . . .

81. Int. Hall.

MASTER OF CEREMONIES: Ladies and gentlemen, pray silence for your Bar Mitzvah Boy, Eliot!

[*Amid applause from the assembled company,* ELIOT *rises to his feet.*

Throughout his speech, cut, as appropriate, to each member of the family, joyfully unaware of any irony.]

ELIOT: My dear mother and father, my dear sister, my dear grandfather, Rabbi Sherman, relatives and friends. On this day that marks my passage from boyhood to manhood, I would like to thank you all for the great honour you have bestowed on me by your presence at this dinnerdance. I shall cherish it all my life without fail. I would like to thank Rabbi Sherman also for the patience he has bestowed on me during the last year while preparing me to learn the portion of the law which I had the honour to recite in the . . . um . . . which I had the honour to recite today. He has been no end of a tower of strength in no uncertain terms. Most of all I would like to thank my dear mother and father for the guidance, wisdom and love which they have bestowed on me during my boyhood. Now that I am a Man, I will follow my dear father's example, and that of my dear grandfather, and last but not least that of my sister Lesley's boyfriend, Harold, in living my life with truth, industry and selfless devotion according to the moral teachings of the Talmud. At the risk of repeating myself they have been no end of a tower of strength in no uncertain terms. I sincerely hope that I will be a credit to them all, and that they will say of me, as Antony did of Brutus in Act 5, scene 5, line 73, 'This was a Man.' Thank you all for the wonderful presents you have bestowed on me of which I am extremely grateful for. I trust you will enjoy your evening, not forgetting the dancing which is about to ensue, as I feel sure you assuredly will. Thank you.

THE END

The Evacuees

First transmission date 5 March 1975

Produced by Mark Shivas
Directed by Alan Parker

SARAH	Maureen Lipman
LOUIS	Ray Mort
MRS GRAHAM	Margery Mason
DANNY	Gary Carp
NEVILLE	Steven Serember
GRANDMA	Margery Withers
ZUCKERMAN	Paul Bestermann
WILHELM	Aubrey Edwards
MR GOLDSTONE	Ian East
MR GRAHAM	Ivor Roberts
PHILIP HYMAN	John Williams
BERNARD	Louis Raynes
MERTON	Laurence Cohen
WORKMAN	Bob West
FIREMAN	Ted Carroll
AMBULANCE MAN	Cyril Varley
OFFICE WOMAN	Christine Buckley
PHOTOGRAPHER	Ray Dunbobbin
MR GROSSFINE	Barron Casenov
MAN IN OVERALLS	Alan Partington
'BANANA WOMAN'	Pat Wallis
FIRST HOUSEWIFE	Gwen Harris
SECOND HOUSEWIFE	Joyce Kennedy
THIRD HOUSEWIFE	Marjorie Sudell
GANG RINGLEADERS	Simon Fish
	George Carleton

1. Ext. Street 'A', Cheetham Hill,
Manchester. Morning.

[*A bleak industrial street – like Derby Street – where the narrow streets of the Jewish quarter begin to widen into the big city streets of town.*
Caption: 'Manchester. September 1st 1939'.
Fade caption on establishing an equally bleak school building, black and forbidding.
Over this, and Scenes 2 and 3, we hear the voice of a teacher, MR GOLDSTONE, *taking the roll-call in his class of 9-year-olds, and the voices of his pupils replying.*]

MR GOLDSTONE [*V.O.*]: Aaron.
AARON [*V.O.*]: Present, Sir.
MR GOLDSTONE [*V.O.*]: Abrahams.
ABRAHAMS [*V.O.*]: Yes, Sir.
MR GOLDSTONE [*V.O.*]: Bergman.
BERGMAN [*V.O.*]: Yes, Sir.
MR GOLDSTONE [*V.O.*]: Bloom.

2. Ext. Street 'A', Cheetham Hill. Morning.

[*An elderly woman –* GRANDMA *– is shuffling speedily down the street. Slightly dotty at the best of times, she's now muttering to herself – agitatedly and tearfully. From time to time she explodes into a sudden angry outburst, then subsides again with a fatalistic shrug of resignation. She's carrying a small brown paper bag.*
Over this, we hear the roll-call continue.]

BLOOM [*V.O.*]: Present, Sir.
MR GOLDSTONE [*V.O.*]: Cohen J.
COHEN J. [*V.O.*]: Yes, Sir.
MR GOLDSTONE [*V.O.*]: Cohen L.

COHEN L. [*V.O.*]: Yes, Sir.

MR GOLDSTONE [*V.O.*]: Cohen S.

[*No reply.*]

Cohen S.

ZUCKERMAN [*V.O.*]: Please Sir, his Mam says to tell you he's feeling bilious.

MR GOLDSTONE [*V.O.*]: Thank you, Zuckerman.

ZUCKERMAN [*V.O.*]: He's probably up to his ears in Kruschen Salts.

MR GOLDSTONE [*V.O.*]: Shut up, Zuckerman.

ZUCKERMAN [*V.O.*]: Yes, Sir.

MR GOLDSTONE [*V.O.*]: Davidson.

3. Ext. School building.

[*With lip trembling Jewishly,* GRANDMA *makes her way towards the entrance of the school, and goes in.*
Over this, the roll-call continues.]

DAVIDSON [*V.O.*]: Present, Sir.

MR GOLDSTONE [*V.O.*]: Gluckman.

GLUCKMAN [*V.O.*]: Yes, Sir.

MR GOLDSTONE [*V.O.*]: Jacobs.

JACOBS [*V.O.*]: Yes, Sir.

MR GOLDSTONE [*V.O.*]: Kestler.

KESTLER [*V.O.*]: Present, Sir.

MR GOLDSTONE [*V.O.*]: Miller.

DANNY [*V.O.*]: Yes, Sir.

4. Int. Classroom. Morning.

[*About twenty boys are seated at their desks. They're all about nine years old and wearing well-worn schoolcaps and raincoats or over-coats. (One or two are coatless and rather more ragged than the rest.) They all have gas-mask cases slung round their shoulders and*

their names on cardboard labels pinned to their lapels. (ZUCKER-
MAN *has no gas-mask case.*)
A youngish teacher – MR GOLDSTONE – *is still taking the roll-
call from his register.*
*The last few names in the roll-call are confirmed by shouts from boys
dotted at random round the class.*]

MR GOLDSTONE: Rabinowitz.

RABINOWITZ: Present, Sir.

MR GOLDSTONE: Schwarz. All right, Schwarz. Tushner.

TUSHNER: Yes, Sir.

MR GOLDSTONE: Wise.

WISE: Yes, Sir.

MR GOLDSTONE: Weisberg.

WEISBERG: Yes, Sir.

MR GOLDSTONE: Winkler.

WINKLER: Yes, Sir.

MR GOLDSTONE: Zuckerman.

ZUCKERMAN: Present and correct, Sir!

MR GOLDSTONE: Where's your gas-mask, Zuckerman?

ZUCKERMAN: Please Sir, I don't know.

MR GOLDSTONE: *Why* don't you know?

ZUCKERMAN: I don't know, Sir.

MR GOLDSTONE: You're a blockhead, Zuckerman. What
are you?

ZUCKERMAN: Please Sir, a blockhead.

[*The rest of the class titters.*]

MR GOLDSTONE: Silence!

[*They promptly fall silent.*

DANNY *continues laughing for a moment, after the others have
stopped. A look from* MR GOLDSTONE *silences him.*]

Now, then. When the bell goes, we all leave the classroom
quietly, and in orderly *fashion,* and walk . . . and when I
say walk I mean walk . . . in single file down to the playground.

[*He looks towards a thin, serious-faced boy slightly older than
the rest, with closely-cropped hair. This is* WILHELM

SCHWARZ, *an Austrian refugee. He wears indoor clothes and has no gas-mask. (Throughout the entire play, he wears a yarmulka.*]

Except you of course, Schwarz.

[WILHELM *nods.*]

Just carry on with your reading exercises, while we're away.

[WILHELM *nods.*

MR GOLDSTONE *resumes his instructions to the rest of the class.*]

Once in the playground, we line up – in *order* – with the rest of the school. Standard One next to the fire escape, then Standard Two, then you lot, then Standard Four and so on.

[*There's a sudden yelp of pain from one of the boys.*]

Yes, Weisberg?

WEISBERG: Please, Sir, someone threw a bean-bag at me! [*He holds the bean-bag as evidence.*]

MR GOLDSTONE [*not looking at* ZUCKERMAN]: Zuckerman, stop throwing bean bags at Weisberg.

ZUCKERMAN [*injured innocence*]: Please, Sir, I never, honest! [MR GOLDSTONE *ignores him and resumes his instructions to the class.*]

MR GOLDSTONE: Once lined up, the whole school – apart from Schwarz here and a few others – will then go *quietly* – and *how* – Zuckerman?

ZUCKERMAN: In orderly fashion, Sir.

MR GOLDSTONE: In orderly fashion – to Cheetham Hill Road, where special trams will be waiting to take us to Victoria Station. We'll get off, line up in single file, then get on again, and come back to school – where Zuckerman will no doubt continue his education by looking at pictures of Desperate Dan eating cow-pie.

[ZUCKERMAN *hastily and guiltily shuts the pages of the comic he's been surreptitiously trying to read.*

The others laugh. The laughter suddenly dies as the door bursts open. Standing in the doorway is GRANDMA – *looking feverishly round the class with tear-filled eyes. Everyone stares at her uncomprehendingly.*]

[*Blankly*] Good morning, Mrs ... er ... Mrs Mendelberg ...

GRANDMA [*absently*]: 'Miller.'

MR GOLDSTONE: Sorry ... 'Miller' ... Um, what exactly ...?

GRANDMA: Where's my ... [*She scans the room and finally catches sight of her grandson, DANNY, and cries tragically*] – Danny!!

[DANNY *sits, embarrassed and perplexed, as she does her shuffling sprint over to him, moaning heartbrokenly.*]

Bubbele! Little Bubbele! They want they should take you away – a fire on their kishkes!

[DANNY, *to his horror, realizes that any second now his* GRANDMA *is going to clutch his head to her breast in front of the entire class. He's right.*

GRANDMA *holds his head against her and rocks to and fro.*]

My shaney little tateleh! Let them take my right arm – that they can have, take, gezuntereit!

[DANNY *silently prays for death.*]

MR GOLDSTONE: Mrs Miller, no one's taking your grandson away.

[GRANDMA *ignores him.*]

GRANDMA [*to* DANNY]: Tateleh ... trains, evacuations – who needs? Stay, darling, be happy. [*To* MR GOLDSTONE *accusingly*] A *baby*, he is!

MR GOLDSTONE [*patiently*]: Mrs Miller. It's a *practice*. Evacuation *practice*. We're going to the station and back. He'll be away an *hour*. Three quarters.

[*None of which* GRANDMA *has listened to. She sobs into* DANNY'S *hair a moment, then turns on* MR GOLDSTONE *again, bitterly.*]

GRANDMA: And you a teacher. Nice. A clever man. Letters behind your name.

[*She nods sadly, ironically, at the enormity of his wickedness, and hugs* DANNY'S *head closer to her breast.*

89

DANNY *hears the tittering of his classmates and shuts his eyes.*]

Every Friday, a lifetime, I chop and fry gefilte fish. You should taste my fish. My fish I could win medals for at the Midland Hotel. Only *this* Friday, how? With *tears*, eppas? And not from the onions – from the *heart*. A baby they take – may they lig in dred. A baby goes to the wars – that's a teacher? That's in library books?

MR GOLDSTONE [*wearily*]: Mrs Miller, there *is* no war. It's a practice in *case* there's a war. There's not even going to be a war. And if there *is* it'll be over by Christmas.

[GRANDMA *looks at him – slowly beginning to understand the situation.*]

GRANDMA: Is a practice?

MR GOLDSTONE: That's all.

GRANDMA: He'll be home tonight, please God?

MR GOLDSTONE: This afternoon.

[*A pause.* GRANDMA *slowly releases* DANNY's *head.*]

GRANDMA: His mother said ... [*Shrugs.*] Ah! ... people talk too quick these days. I'll go, gezuntereit. [*Sharply to* DANNY] Sit nice, like a mensch.

[DANNY *sits up correctly.*]

Put your cap straight. [*She straightens it for him.*] Better. [*Pause, then quietly*] I'd made you a piece fried fish for the travelling. [*She plonks the brown paper bag on his desk and exits.*]

5. Ext. Street 'B', Cheetham Hill.
Early evening.

[*A dingy street in the heart of the Jewish quarter.*
DANNY *and his twelve-year-old brother,* NEVILLE, *are playing marbles with two or three other kids in the road and gutter. One of the boys is called* ALEC.
A few yards away, watching them, is WILHELM, *leaning against a wall, hands in pockets.*

Two girls are playing with whips and tops nearby.
The boys play for a moment, rowdily, then NEVILLE *notices*
WILHELM.]

NEVILLE: Want a game?
  [WILHELM *shakes his head.*]
  Did you play alleys in Austria?
  [WILHELM *shrugs to indicate he doesn't know.*
  An older boy, MERTON, *about fifteen years old, passes,*
  wearing ordinary clothes apart from heavy football boots and
  his trousers tucked into his socks. He bounces an old leather
  football in front of him as he walks. DANNY *watches his*
  approach with hero-worshipping eyes.]
  Hello, Merton.
MERTON [*cool*]: Howdo.
DANNY: Hello, Merton.
MERTON [*amiably*]: Tiddler.
  [*He continues on his way.*
  DANNY *watches.*]
DANNY: He's one of the best dribblers in England, isn't he,
  Merton?
NEVILLE: He's O.K.
DANNY: He'll play for Wolves when he's grown up. Any
  money.
ALEC: Why the Wolves?
DANNY: Any money, he will. It's irrelevant.
ALEC: Why not City or the Rags?
NEVILLE: He supports the Wolves, our kid. He likes the
  name.
ALEC: He's barmy.
DANNY: Why am I?
ALEC: Wolves can't play for toffee.
NEVILLE [*to* DANNY]: Hit him.
DANNY [*a touch scared*]: I will in a minute.
ALEC: Yeah? You and whose army?
DANNY: Shurrup you!
ALEC: What if I don't?

NEVILLE [*to* DANNY]: Bash his head in.

DANNY [*evasively*]: Look, I thought we was playing alleys!

ALEC: You're scared.

DANNY: Who is?

ALEC: You is.

[NEVILLE *grabs* ALEC *and pins him to the ground, then turns to* DANNY.]

NEVILLE: Go on, our kid! Now! Thump him!

DANNY [*evasively*]: I might. I might not.

[NEVILLE *releases* ALEC.]

NEVILLE: It's all right, Alec, he wouldn't. [*Amused.*] Going to be a rabbi, aren't you, Danny?

[*He laughs.*

DANNY *promptly hurls himself at* NEVILLE. NEVILLE *trots off up the street, laughing and handing off* DANNY, *who's pursuing him – raining ineffectual punches.*]

[*While dodging*] What sort of job's that for a Yiddishe boy?

6. Int. The Millers' living room.
(*Continuous in time.*)

[*The house and furniture are very working-class.*
Open on GRANDMA *lighting the two Sabbath candles and saying the prayer.*
SARAH – DANNY *and* NEVILLE's *mother – is laying the table for dinner. She's a blonde.*
LOUIS – *the boys' father – is polishing his boots by the fire.*]

GRANDMA: Boruch atto adonai Elohanu melech ho-oulom. Asher kidashonu b'mitzvousov. Votzeevonu. L'chadlik nair shel-shabbos.

[*She starts to light the candles.*

SARAH *is placing a big bowl of soup on to the table.*]

SARAH [*to* LOUIS]: Every since I got home from work ... Sticking her finger in the soup, sucking it, saying 'It needs more salt'. Then sticking it back in again ...

GRANDMA [*to* SARAH *and* LOUIS, *as she finishes lighting the candles*]: Good shabbos.

    [LOUIS *hands* SARAH *his pay-packet.*]

LOUIS: Fruits of my labours.

SARAH [*looking at the amount on the back of the packet*]: Two pound ten...??

GRANDMA: I said 'Good shabbos'.

LOUIS: Things are slack everywhere. They're worried there'll be a war... [*to* GRANDMA] Good shabbos.

SARAH: How do we manage on two pound ten?

LOUIS: Two pound seven and six. I owed half a dollar union money.

GRANDMA [*pointedly to* SARAH]: I said 'Good shabbos'.

SARAH: I know. [*She sighs.*] Good shabbos. I'll get·the kids in.

    [*She starts to exit to the hall.*

    GRANDMA *dips her finger into the soup, sucks it and grimaces.*]

GRANDMA [*to* LOUIS]: It needed more salt...

SARAH [*shouting from the door*]: It got more salt!

    [GRANDMA, *chastened, dips her finger in again and sucks it.*]

GRANDMA: Mmmm! [*appreciatively*] Believe me, I can tell! [*to* LOUIS] Beautiful!

7. Ext. Street 'B', Cheetham Hill.
(*Continuous in time.*)

[NEVILLE *still teasingly avoiding* DANNY'S *flailing fists.* SARAH *appears at the doorway, and calls.*]

SARAH: Danny! Neville! Dinner!

NEVILLE: In a sec.

SARAH: Now!

DANNY: Our kid's got to win his blood-alley back!

SARAH: Are you asking for a good hiding, the pair of you?

    [NEVILLE *and* DANNY *start off back to the house and pass*

*a couple of workmen who are cutting iron railings from outside
the houses and loading them on to a horse and cart.*]

DANNY: Where are they taking the railings?

WORKMAN: For munitions. In case war breaks out.

DANNY: Railings? ? ?

[NEVILLE *calls to* WILHELM *who's still watching.*]

NEVILLE: We're going in now.

[WILHELM *nods and shrugs.*

NEVILLE *picks up the marbles.*]

Ta, ra.

[WILHELM *shyly nods acknowledgement and wanders off in
the opposite direction.*]

DANNY: He gives me the creeps, Wilhelm . . .

[*He and* NEVILLE *start off towards their house.*]

SARAH [*calling from the door*]: Come on! You'll have it dark!

[DANNY *turns and calls back to the workman.*]

DANNY: Mr Goldstone at school says there isn't going to *be*
no war!

[*They walk on till they reach the door.*]

SARAH: Look at your knees! Like baitsommer!

[DANNY *and* NEVILLE *automatically guard their heads
with their arms as they dash past their mother's threatening
raised hand and into the hall. The threat isn't carried out.*
SARAH *follows them in and closes the door behind herself.*]

8. Int. Mr Grossfine's shop. Day.

[MR GROSSFINE *is serving* DANNY *with the family's Sunday
morning bagels.*]

9. Ext. school building. Day.

[*Over Scenes 8 and 9, we hear the voice of* NEVILLE CHAMBER-
LAIN *in his radio broadcast of 3 September 1939, announcing the
declaration of war.*]

CHAMBERLAIN [*V.O.*]: This morning, the British Ambassador in Berlin handed the German Government a note, stating that unless we heard from them by eleven o'clock, that they were prepared to withdraw their troops from Poland, a state of war would exist between us. I have to tell you now that no such undertaking has been received, and that consequently this country is at war with Germany.

> [*Overlay the end of the above on to the opening of Scene 10, mixing the sound into the beginning of* MR GOLDSTONE's *roll-call.*]

10. Int. Classroom. Morning.

[*The class is seated as before, except that now each boy has a labelled haversack or suitcase on top of his desk. (All except* WILHELM, *who has no coat or case.*)
MR GOLDSTONE *stands before them – in hat and coat – holding a clipboard of papers detailing evacuation procedure.*
Everyone is now serious – some of the boys pale and apprehensive. Solemn.
As opposed to his earlier scenes, MR GOLDSTONE *is rather gravely brisk and purposeful. He's calling the roll from the register.*]

MR GOLDSTONE: Weisberg.
WEISBERG: Present.
MR GOLDSTONE: Winkler.
WINKLER: Present.
MR GOLDSTONE: Zuckerman.
ZUCKERMAN: Present.
MR GOLDSTONE: Got your gas-mask, Zuckerman?
ZUCKERMAN: Yes, Sir.
MR GOLDSTONE: Now, pay attention, all of you. When the bell goes, into the playground. Line up next to Standard Two. Then – tram, then – railway station. Parents will see you off at the platform ... Any brothers from other

Standards will travel with you. When we get to Blackpool, you'll all be issued with – given, that is – a tin of corned beef. Then we'll set off and try and find . . . get you fixed up with foster-parents in either Blackpool or St Annes.' Right. Stand up.

[*They all stand up, except* WILHELM. MR GOLDSTONE *notices him.*]

Oh. Sorry, Schwarz. You may as well go home now. Tomorrow morning, go to Mr Davidson's class. You'll all be in the same class – all those not being evacuated. All right?

[WILHELM *nods.*]

And I'll see you soon and the Dead-End kids here'll see you as soon as we've won the war. Off you go, lad.

[WILHELM *makes his way to the door. He glances awkwardly at the row of boys as he goes. He looks at* DANNY. DANNY *nods and smiles briefly.* WILHELM *stiffly makes to shake* DANNY's *hand – but* DANNY *doesn't understand what he's expected to do.* WILHELM *embarrassedly withdraws his hand.*

ZUCKERMAN *sniggers.*

WILHELM *exits.*

The school bell abruptly rings.]

All got your luggage?

[*The boys heave their haversacks and cases.*]

Right, now first row lead off and – oh! one more thing. Some of you – *most* of you – will be going to people who aren't Jewish. The food won't be kosher. Now, it doesn't matter. It isn't a sin. There's a war on. Try and remember to put your tzizit on every morning. Now first row – quietly –

[*The first row starts to file towards the door.*]

11. Ext. Railway carriage. Victoria Station.
        Morning.

[SARAH, DANNY and NEVILLE – *amid a crush of other mothers
and children – struggling to board the train. Much noise, bustle and
chaos.*]

12. Int. Railway carriage. Victoria Station.
        Morning.

[*A chaos of bustling activity. A few boys – including* DANNY *and*
NEVILLE– *are organizing themselves for the journey. There's a
tremendous hubbub of noise – mostly caused by several mothers
helping their sons get their haversacks on to the luggage racks and
straightening their dishevelled caps, ties and socks.*
SARAH *is attending to* DANNY *and* NEVILLE. *Throughout the
scene she's very close to tears – but trying to hide it, not altogether
successfully, beneath a determined calmness and conviviality.*]

SARAH: And I'll get your address from Mr Goldstone first
    thing in the morning – and I'll be over to see you Satur-
    day afternoon. Yes? So it's not long, is it? Till Saturday?
DANNY [*quietly*]: How long will you stay?
SARAH: Till Sunday night. A whole day and a half.
NEVILLE: When will you come again?
SARAH: Every two or three weeks. Month at the most.
    When I can afford. [*To cover her emotion, she busies herself
    with their appearance – including spitting on her hanky then
    rubbing their faces with it. Which is something kids don't like –
    it hurts more than you think.*] And I'll write letters. And you
    will. It'll be like a holiday.
DANNY: Mam, I don't think I want to go, Mam.
    [*We hear whistles from the guard on the platform.*]
SARAH: And be good boys to your new ... to the people
    that take you in, and ...

97

DANNY: I'm fed up being evacuated, I hate it.

[GRANDMA's *face suddenly becomes visible through the open window of the carriage.*]

GRANDMA: You're such an expert – what you hate, what you don't hate! Blackpool's like the seaside.

NEVILLE: It *is* the seaside!

GRANDMA [*to* DANNY]: See! Listen to your brother.

SARAH: Now, you will write? Tonight? As soon as you've –

GRANDMA: Sarah – let them go, gezuntereit.

[*Both women, tears very imminent, look at the two boys.*]

Cheeky little chazars – it'll be a holiday *without* them, believe me!

[SARAH *opens the door and gets out on to the platform, turning her head away so that the boys can't see her distress.*

GRANDMA *takes the opportunity to pass a brown paper bag through the window to the boys, surreptitiously.*]

A little chopped liver for the travelling . . .

13. Ext. Platform.

[SARAH *catches* GRANDMA *handing over the paper bag.*]

SARAH: You've never gone and –

GRANDMA: Come on, Sarah. God's good. It's better. Away from the bombs.

14. Int. Railway carriage.

[DANNY *and* NEVILLE *sit looking out at* SARAH *and* GRAND-MA. NEVILLE *holds the paper bag.*

The noise and bustle have dissipated. Suddenly, sharply, we hear the guard's whistle. The train moves off.]

15. Ext. Platform.

[SARAH *and* GRANDMA *stand and watch the train begin to pull away and gather speed. They turn and start to walk back down the platform.*]

16. Ext. Promenade. Blackpool.

[DANNY's *class led by* MR GOLDSTONE, *walk in profile along the promenade then turn inland.*]

17. Ext. Blackpool, street 'A'. Afternoon.

[*Coming up the street – away from the promenade (indicated, perhaps, by a promenade 'pagoda' shelter) is most of* DANNY's *class, led by* MR GOLDSTONE, *and including* NEVILLE.
They walk up the residential street, in a crocodile, each boy carrying a tin of corned beef, as well as his case (or haversack) and gas-mask case. Some of them are fitfully singing 'Ten Green Bottles' or 'Michael Finnegan'.
ZUCKERMAN *is wearing his gas-mask.*]

18. Ext. Blackpool, street 'B'.

[*The crocodile of boys walk along,* ZUCKERMAN *still wearing his gas-mask.*
An air-raid siren begins to wail. The boys look up at the sky, apprehensively. The singing stops.]

MR GOLDSTONE: It's not an air-raid. They're just trying the sirens out. They do it every afternoon. It's a practice.
NEVILLE [*to* DANNY]: We've heard *that* one before.
DANNY: Yes, he can tell that to the marines, can't he?

[*Hoping for appreciation.*] I said he can tell that to the marines, didn't I?

[*The crocodile comes to a halt, while* MR GOLDSTONE *enters a garden gate and starts up the path to a house.*

At the window of the neighbouring house, a woman's face appears at the parted curtain, looks horrified at the boys, and disappears again, as the curtains are closed.

MR GOLDSTONE *rings the doorbell of her neighbour.*]

MR GOLDSTONE [*without looking round*]: Take it off, Zuckerman.

[ZUCKERMAN *takes off his gas-mask.*

The door opens and a young HOUSEWIFE *appears. She takes in the scene, suspiciously.*]

Good afternoon, madam. My name is Mr Goldstone. I'm a teacher from . . .

FIRST HOUSEWIFE [*hastily*]: I can't take no evacuees!

MR GOLDSTONE: Oh.

FIRST HOUSEWIFE [*guiltily*]; I'd like to. Only . . . um . . . [*she tries to think of an excuse.*] Only I have this invalid father. Sorry.

[MR GOLDSTONE *smiles his acknowledgement. She closes the door, and he returns to his charges. They start to tramp off to the next house.*]

DANNY: I hate Her Hitler. [*'Her' mispronounced as written.*]

NEVILLE [*correcting him*]: 'Herr' Hitler.

DANNY: What?

NEVILLE: It's 'Herr' not 'Her'.

DANNY [*defeated*]: Sometimes, it's Her.

NEVILLE: Never.

DANNY: It can be. It's irrelevant.

[*Cut to* MR GOLDSTONE *at the next door, talking to* SECOND HOUSEWIFE.]

SECOND HOUSEWIFE: Sorry, I only wish I could. [*Thinks for a moment.*] Only I have three of my own, you see. Well, four, really.

MR GOLDSTONE: Three or four?

SECOND HOUSEWIFE: Four. All told. It wouldn't be doing right by them.

MR GOLDSTONE: Thank you madam. Good day.

SECOND HOUSEWIFE: Not at all. Pleasure to be of help. [*She closes the door.*]

19. Ext. Blackpool, street 'C'.

[*A couple of hours later.*
The crocodile is now somewhat shorter – and much more weary. The boys trudge along either dragging their cases or bent double by their haversacks – still clutching their tins of corned beef.
Cut to MR GOLDSTONE *talking to* THIRD HOUSEWIFE *on her doorstep.*

THIRD HOUSEWIFE [*surveying the boys doubtfully*]: Are they clean?

MR GOLDSTONE [*wearily*]: Oh, yes, madam. We have to evacuate the cleanest first, by Act of Parliament.

THIRD HOUSEWIFE: What?

MR GOLDSTONE: They're all very clean.

THIRD HOUSEWIFE: Go on, then. I'll try one.

MR GOLDSTONE: Thank you, madam. Which?
[*She stands, surveying the boys – like a cattle market.*
The boys stand looking back at her – some thrusting their chests and faces forward hoping to be chosen, others too tired and past caring.
ZUCKERMAN *pulls his tongue at her.*]

THIRD HOUSEWIFE: That one. [*She points to* NEVILLE.]

MR GOLDSTONE: Sorry. He's one of a pair.

THIRD HOUSEWIFE: Eh?

MR GOLDSTONE: He's with his brother. We try not to separate brothers.

THIRD HOUSEWIFE: I can't take *two* . . .

MR GOLDSTONE: Can I interest you in one of the others perhaps?

THIRD HOUSEWIFE: He'll do.

> [*She points at* WINKLER.
>
> MR GOLDSTONE *pushes* WINKLER *to her and gives them both thick sheaves of paper bearing typed instructions and advice.*]

MR GOLDSTONE: Say hello to the lady.

WINKLER: Hello.

MR GOLDSTONE [*while writing down the woman's address on his clipboard*]: This is Cyril Winkler.

THIRD HOUSEWIFE [*to* WINKLER]: That's a funny name, isn't it?

MR GOLDSTONE: Say yes.

WINKLER: Yes.

THIRD HOUSEWIFE [*pulling* WINKLER'S *shirt collar down slightly*]: Got a tide-mark as well, haven't you? [*She ushers him in and closes the door*].

20. Ext. Blackpool, street 'D'. Dusk.

[*All that's left of the crocodile is* MR GOLDSTONE, DANNY, NEVILLE *and* ZUCKERMAN. *All desperately weary, hungry and footsore.*

The three boys are sitting on their haversacks on the pavement, while MR GOLDSTONE *is negotiating – with a middle-aged housewife,* MRS GRAHAM, *at her doorway.*]

DANNY: I think being evacuated stinks.

ZUCKERMAN: Wilhelm Schwarz had more sense.

NEVILLE: You barm-pot! He's got foster-parents already, in Manchester!

DANNY: They said he's done enough running, Mr Goldstone said. That's why they wouldn't let him come.

ZUCKERMAN: What if the Germans get him, though? They shot his real mam and dad in Austria, didn't they?

DANNY: Czechoslovakia.

ZUCKERMAN: Austria.

DANNY: Czechoslovakia, wasn't it, our kid?

NEVILLE: No, Austria.

DANNY [*defeated*]: I meant Austria, clever! [*Pause.*] The Czechoslovakian part.

[*A tired pause.*]

ZUCKERMAN: Why doesn't Wilhelm never talk? He never ever says anything. Not even at playtime even.

[*Another weary silence.*]

DANNY: Being evacuated's the worst thing in the world. It's worse than being buried up to your neck by Fuzzy-Wuzzies in the desert so's the ants get you.

ZUCKERMAN: What's next worse?

DANNY: There isn't one.

[*They all think for a moment.*]

ZUCKERMAN: What about if the Clay Men in Flash Gordon get you?

[MR GOLDSTONE *calls from the doorway.*]

MR GOLDSTONE: The Miller Boys! Come here!

[DANNY *and* NEVILLE *jerk an apprehensive look to the doorway.*]

This is Mrs Graham. She's taking you.

NEVILLE [*picking up his haversack*]: Ta, ra, Zuckie.

DANNY [*picking up his haversack*]: See you tomorrow.

ZUCKERMAN: I bet she's a witch. Any money.

[NEVILLE *takes* DANNY'*s haversack from him, so that he can hold his brother's hand as they go up the path to the doorway.*

MR GOLDSTONE *gives them their papers.*

Cut back to ZUCKERMAN, *sitting on his haversack, waiting.*

MR GOLDSTONE *joins him.*]

MR GOLDSTONE [*sighing wearily*]: Come on, Hopalong Cassidy.

[ZUCKERMAN *gets up, hoists up his haversack and they start tramping off together down the street.*]

ZUCKERMAN: There's no houses *left*.

MR GOLDSTONE: There's thousands.

[*They walk on.*]

ZUCKERMAN: Please sir, can I go back to Manchester?
MR GOLDSTONE: No.
[*He strides on.* ZUCKERMAN *trundles along behind him.*]
ZUCKERMAN: I've got a headache in my leg.

21. Int. Mrs Graham's hallway.

[DANNY *and* NEVILLE *stand in the hall, their caps on their heads, their luggage at their feet. They stand for a moment or two, looking at each other, nonplussed.*]

DANNY: She's scrammed!
NEVILLE: She went up the dancers.
DANNY: What for?
NEVILLE: *I* don't know!
DANNY: Has she gone to bed?
[*They stand there. Small. Lonely.*
The bathroom door at the top of the stairs opens, we hear the sound of running water. MRS GRAHAM *appears at the bathroom door.*]
MRS GRAHAM: Come along, children. A nice hot bath.
NEVILLE: We had a bath on Sunday.
MRS GRAHAM: Upstairs please, like big boys.
[*She goes back inside.*
They start upstairs.]

22. Int. Mrs Graham's lounge/dining room. Evening.

[*The house and furniture are comfortably middle-class.*
MRS GRAHAM *is preparing the table for tea.*
MR GRAHAM *is in an armchair listening to Hitler giving a speech —*
punctuated by a chorus of thousands shouting 'Sieg Heil!' on the wireless. From time to time MR GRAHAM *shakes his head sadly and sighs.*]

DANNY *and* NEVILLE *enter from upstairs, scrubbed clean after their exhausting day, wearing identical fair-isle pullovers, and their school caps.*

DANNY *stops dead on hearing Hitler's voice – and on seeing* MR GRAHAM *listening to it. He at once suspects him of being a German spy. He glances at* NEVILLE, *who understands but dismisses the theory with an impatient shake of the head.*

MRS GRAHAM *looks at them.*]

MRS GRAHAM: Oh! No caps, children! Not indoors.

NEVILLE: We've always worn them.

MRS GRAHAM: I don't think so. [*She takes their caps off.*]

MRS GRAHAM: To the table, children. [*To* MR GRAHAM] Tea, dear?

MR GRAHAM: Atta girl!

[*He switches the wireless off, makes his way to the table and sits down.*

MRS GRAHAM *also sits down – in the only remaining chair.*

The two boys look blankly at the table, wondering where they're supposed to sit. Two plates have been laid for them – each bearing one cold sausage – but no chairs.

MR GRAHAM *bows his head in prayer.* MRS GRAHAM *likewise.*

The two boys stand at the table facing their plate of cold sausage.]

MR GRAHAM: For what we're about to receive, may the Lord make us truly thankful. Amen. [*He digs into his meal.*]

MRS GRAHAM: Amen. [*To the boys*] 'Amen'.

NEVILLE: Amen.

MRS GRAHAM: Danny?

DANNY: Amen – what is it?

MRS GRAHAM: 'What is it, Mrs Graham?'

DANNY [*confused*]: What? [*Looks down at the sausage.*]

MRS GRAHAM: Silly lad. It's a sausage.

NEVILLE [*to* MRS GRAHAM]: Shall we stand here?

MRS GRAHAM: You boys like football?

DANNY: Yes.

MRS GRAHAM: 'Yes, Mrs Graham.'

NEVILLE [*to* DANNY]: You've to say 'Mrs Graham' at the end of the sentence. [*To* MR GRAHAM] Sometimes, Mr Graham.

MR GRAHAM: I watch Blackpool now and then. Top of the first division. Saw them wallop the Wolves on Saturday. [*Which doesn't please* DANNY.] Two-one. Jock Dodds got both.

DANNY: I don't like cold sausage, Mrs Graham.

MRS GRAHAM: Of course you do! It's real pork.

[DANNY *and* NEVILLE *exchange an immediate frantic glance of panic. Real pork is the biggest crisis they've ever had to face.*]

NEVILLE: Is there anything else instead, Mrs Graham?

MRS GRAHAM: [*putting down her knife and fork*] Neville. One thing I shall not entertain. And that's impertinence. Mr Graham and I like little boys who are grateful for being taken off the streets and given a home. [*She continues eating.*]

NEVILLE: Could we have the corned beef we brought – do you think – Mrs Graham?

MRS GRAHAM: No. That stays in the larder for when there's a shortage.

DANNY: We've never had pork sausage, Mrs Graham. We're not allowed it.

MR GRAHAM [*with consummate wisdom*]: How do you know you don't like it, then, eh? Mmmmm? Can't answer that one, can you? Eh, boys? Blinded by science, eh?

MRS GRAHAM [*to the boys, annoyed*]: Just don't know there's a war *on*, do you.

[MR *and* MRS GRAHAM *continue eating their meal.*

DANNY *and* NEVILLE *look at each other.*

NEVILLE *realizes he has to take the lead and make a decision. He struggles through a little crisis of conscience, then cuts a small piece of his sausage – whispers a short Hebrew prayer to himself – hand on head – and eats.*

DANNY *watches. Accepts the decision and puts his hand on his head to whisper the Hebrew prayer.*]

MRS GRAHAM *glances at him. He pretends he's scratching his head, then drops his hand and eats.*]

23. Int. The Millers' living room. Evening.

[*Open on* DANNY's *and* NEVILLE's *empty chairs at the table.* GRANDMA, SARAH *and* LOUIS *are seated in their chairs at the table, having their evening meal. They eat in unaccustomed silence, each of them upset at the boys' absence . . . and each aware of what the others are feeling.*]

GRANDMA: So have you both gone stumm or something? Suddenly no one talks all of a sudden!
[SARAH *tries to think of something to talk about.*]
SARAH [*gently*]: Is the soup salty enough for you? [*No response.*] We'll go round Hightown tomorrow, eh? Get some blackout curtains.
[*No response.* SARAH *racks her brains for another topic of conversation.*]
SARAH: Louis starts fire-watching next week, don't you, Louis? [*Pause.*] Watching for fires. [*Pause.*] Two nights a week. In case there's –
GRANDMA: Sarah, Yachny-divossy, do me a favour, stop talking. Eh? Thank you.

24. Int. The boys' bedroom. Night.

[DANNY *and* NEVILLE *are lying back to back in bed – both tired but awake. Faintly, from downstairs, we hear on the wireless 'Monday night at 8.00 o'clock'. The boys are silent for a few moments. Looking into space, mulling over the events of the day.*]

DANNY: If he isn't a spy, why was he listening to Her Hitler?
NEVILLE: *Herr* Hitler. He isn't. Go to sleep.

DANNY: Your big fat elbow's only sticking in my ribs.

[NEVILLE *shifts position slightly. Tears imminent.*]

Neville . . .

NEVILLE: Go to sleep.

DANNY: It'll be over by Christmas, won't it? Any money?

NEVILLE: 'Course.

DANNY: We'll write to Mam tomorrow. [*Pause.*] Railings can't do much against *tanks*. You can only make spears out of railings.

[*A long pause. They seem to be settling down to sleep. We hear* DANNY *quietly sobbing to himself.*

NEVILLE *listens to him – fighting back his own tears.*]

NEVILLE: We'll be all right.

[DANNY *continues sobbing.*]

Sssshhh.

[DANNY *continues sobbing.*

NEVILLE *gets up on one elbow and belts his brother across the head.*]

Now, shurrup!!

[DANNY *quietens down. A pause.*]

DANNY: I forgot to say my prayers.

NEVILLE: Do you want another good hiding?

[DANNY *whispers his prayers to himself.*]

DANNY: Boruch atto adonai Elohanu melech ho'oulom. Hamapeel chevlai . . . er . . . [*He's lost. He tries again.*] Hamapeel chevlai . . . er . . . [*Lost again. Tries again.*] . . . Hamapeel chevlai shano, al anai . . . er . . . al anai . . . [*He gives up and continues in English.*] Blessed are Thou O Lord Our God, King of the Universe. Please look after Mam and Dad and everyone, and let Hitler get a railing up his tochass. Amen.

25. Ext. Waterproof garment factory.
Manchester. Morning.

[LOUIS *and* SARAH *walking briskly along the street, going to work. He wears a cloth cap, she a turban.*]

SARAH [*V.O.*]: 'Dear Neville and Danny . . . Just a line to let you know all is well at this end. Your dad's chest is better, he says, now that he's back on the Woodbines. He says at this rate he'll be after Frank Swift's job in the City goal. Joke.'

26. Int. Factory. Day.

[LOUIS *is at his bench, varnishing mackintosh sleeves to the body of the coat. At other benches, men of* LOUIS' *age are working. One of these is* BERNARD.

SARAH *passes carrying a high pile of cut-out sleeves to another bench.*]

SARAH [*V.O.*]: 'We're both busy at work, where everyone says the war will definitely be over soon, as the Germans are without butter and starving.'

   [*A* WOMAN *from the 'office' approaches distributing pay-packets from a tray. She hands* LOUIS *his. He immediately looks at the details on the back.*]

LOUIS: A pound??

WOMAN: A pound clear. You had a dead horse to work off from *last* week.

LOUIS: How the hell do we manage on a pound?

WOMAN: The manager says we'll be on Government orders soon. Tons of work. Army coats, capes, everything. Be like the good old days.

BERNARD: When were *they*, sweetheart?

27. Ext. Street 'B', Cheetham Hill. Day.

[WILHELM *desultorily playing marbles, alone, where he watched the boys playing marbles earlier.*

SARAH *approaches, carrying shopping bag.*]

SARAH [*V.O.*]: 'It's pretty quiet on the street these days, without you and the other boys fighting, and breaking windows. But we're getting used to it.'

[*She smiles at* WILHELM.]

Hello.

[WILHELM *lowers his eyes.*

SARAH *offers him a chocolate bar from her shopping bag.*]

Buzz Bar?

[WILHELM *shakes his head and moves away.*

SARAH *smiles and continues towards her house.*]

[*V.O.*] 'And I had a nice long chat with that foreign boy today, Wilhelm, who sends you his regards.'

28. Ext. Street 'C', Cheetham Hill. Day.

[SARAH *passes* MERTON *who's leaning against a wall, blowing up a football with a bicycle pump. She smiles at him. He watches her ankles as she walks on. He gives her a wolf whistle. She looks back quietly amused and walks on.*]

SARAH [*V.O.*]: 'Not forgetting Merton, the footballer, who's getting quite a big boy now.'

29. Int. The Millers' living room. Night.

[GRANDMA *is asleep in the chair, mouth hanging wide open, her prayer book still in her hand.*

SARAH *is seated at the table writing her letter. On the table, ready to be parcelled up, are a cooked chicken and the other items she mentions.*]

SARAH [*V.O.*]: 'I'm enclosing a cooked chicken with helzel, and some marzipan cake, and two chocolate Buzz Bars. And a balaclava helmet each I've knitted. They're both the same, so no fighting.'

[*The sirens start wailing.*]

'Your grandma is with me at the time of writing.'

[*She glances across at* GRANDMA *who's now snoring.*]

'. . . and sends her love. She was listening to Lord Haw-Haw on the wireless yesterday – and said she knows who he really is. Guess who? Jack Buchanan acting the goat! Anyway, that's all for now. I'll be over to see you soon, and be good boys to Mr and Mrs Graham. Lots of love, and keep warm. Pip, pip, pip. Your loving Mam and Dad.'

A.R.P. WARDEN [*O.O.V.*]: Put that bloody light out!

[SARAH *gets up, switches the light off, and by the light of the fire, pops the letter into a cardboard box – into which she starts parcelling the food.*]

30. Int. Mrs Graham's kitchen. Morning.

[*On the table is the parcel* SARAH *sent – now opened.* MRS GRAHAM *is reading* SARAH'S *letter. She then stuffs it into her apron pocket and exits towards the lounge.*]

31. Int. Mrs Graham's lounge.
(Continuous in time.)

[DANNY *and* NEVILLE *are reluctantly polishing the furniture.*]

DANNY: We'll be late for school!

NEVILLE: Tell us one we don't know, clever!

[*They continue polishing for a moment.*]

DANNY: We're always late!

NEVILLE: Shurrup – or we'll have more to do tonight.

[MRS GRAHAM *enters from the kitchen.*

DANNY *and* NEVILLE *at once start polishing furiously.*]

MRS GRAHAM: Boys – there's been a letter from your mother.

[*They stop work and look up at her expectantly.*]

Everyone's very well at home, and she hopes you're both being good boys.

[*She smiles at them good-humouredly.*]

And you are, aren't you? Specially when you're asleep! Do you get it?

NEVILLE: Please can we read it – the letter?

DANNY [*finishing* NEVILLE'S *sentence for him*]: Mrs Graham?

MRS GRAHAM: Oh, I didn't think. I've thrown it away now. But she's sent you a nice parcel.

DANNY [*hopeful excitement*]: Stuff to eat??

MRS GRAHAM: Two lovely balaclavas to keep your ears cosy. So she hasn't forgotten you, has she?

[*The boys swallow their disappointment.*]

Have you written to *her*, this week?

[DANNY *looks at* NEVILLE *for guidance.* NEVILLE *stares ahead, lips sealed.*]

Remember your mother said you'd to be good.

[*Another tiny hesitation, then* DANNY *takes a letter from his pocket, before* NEVILLE *can stop him.*]

DANNY: We just need an envelope.

MRS GRAHAM: I'll get one for you. And post it.

[*She grabs the letter from him, and starts scanning through its pages, as she exits to the kitchen.*

DANNY *frustratedly realizes he's been conned. His eyes look as though they're about to fill up again.* NEVILLE *swiftly belts him one.*]

32. Ext. Blackpool promenade. Afternoon.

[*A small squad of R.A.F. recruits are being drilled by their instructor.*

NEVILLE, DANNY *and* ZUCKERMAN, *each carrying his satchel, pass by – showing no interest in the R.A.F. men (they've seen similar sights many times before).* DANNY *is running his Dinky Toy racing car along the rail. As he walks:*]

ZUCKERMAN: Why don't you kill her?

NEVILLE: How?

ZUCKERMAN: Sabotage. Shoot her with a tommy-gun.

NEVILLE: You're barmy, you!

> [*There's a pause.*
>
> DANNY *and* NEVILLE *are very morose.*
>
> ZUCKERMAN *is trying to decide whether to confess a secret. He finally decides he will.*]

ZUCKERMAN [*quietly*]: I'm going to escape.

> [DANNY *and* NEVILLE *look at him, puzzled but impressed. They stop walking.*]

I'm going home. Back to Manchester.

DANNY: When?

ZUCKERMAN: Soon.

NEVILLE: How?

ZUCKERMAN: I've got a secret plan.

DANNY: What is it?

ZUCKERMAN: I haven't just worked it out yet.

> [*They stand silently, preoccupied.*
>
> DANNY *looks at* NEVILLE *to see if the thought of escape interests him.*
>
> NEVILLE *starts off towards home.*
>
> ZUCKERMAN *starts off the other way.*
>
> DANNY *starts following* NEVILLE.]

[*Turning*] Do you want to come in on it?

DANNY [*promptly*]: Yes!!

NEVILLE [*reluctantly*]: No.

DANNY: Go on, our kid!

NEVILLE: I said no!

> [ZUCKERMAN *walks on.*]

DANNY [*muttering behind* NEVILLE]: We might. You never know. It's only irrelevant.

> [*They walk on.*]

33. Ext. Sand dunes 'A', South Shore.
A little later on.

[DANNY, *with great interest, and* NEVILLE, *against his will, are surreptitiously trailing a teenage girl across the dunes.*]

NEVILLE: You don't know what 'irrelevant' even means.
DANNY: I do!
NEVILLE: What then?
DANNY [*evasively*]: Just 'cos *you* don't . . .
    [*The girl descends into a hollow between the dunes.*
    DANNY *and* NEVILLE *creep to the brow of the dune and peer over.*
    The girl runs to a young soldier who's sitting there waiting for her. They go into a clinch.
    DANNY *and* NEVILLE *turn away disappointed.*]
NEVILLE: I told you she wasn't a spy.
    [*They walk on.*]

34. Ext. Sand dunes 'B', South Shore.
A little later.

[DANNY *and* NEVILLE *are still walking home.*
We suddenly hear a piercing sound, like the mating-call of a bird whose voice is breaking.
NEVILLE *stops dead in his tracks.*
Other calls – many other calls – come from different directions, replying to the first.
NEVILLE *takes* DANNY'*s arm. They stand looking round.*
From their P.O.V. we pan round the grassy tops of the dunes which surround them, in a full circle.
DANNY *and* NEVILLE *are now both very alarmed.*
Suddenly, from behind each dune, a small boy steps forward. They all begin to converge on DANNY *and* NEVILLE *in a circle. They stop a yard or so away and their* RINGLEADER *steps forward.*]

RINGLEADER: Where are *you* going then?

NEVILLE: Nowhere.

RINGLEADER: It's *our* say who goes across here. What gang are you in?

NEVILLE: We're not in any.

RINGLEADER [*suspiciously*]: You're not from round here, are you?

NEVILLE: Manchester. [*Pronounced 'Manchister'.*]

RINGLEADER: Where??

DANNY: Manchester. [*Pronounced 'Manchister'.*]

[*The* RINGLEADER *turns to his gang, laughing.*]

RINGLEADER: They can't even *say* it right! [*To* DANNY *and* NEVILLE] It's Manchester, not Manchister!

[*His gang laughs.*]

Isn't it?

DANNY: Yes. [*Pronounced 'Yis'.*]

[*The* RINGLEADER *again roars with laughter. His gang join in.*]

RINGLEADER: Do you want us to let you go?

DANNY: Yes. [*Pronounced 'Yis'.*]

[*The gang roars with laughter.*]

RINGLEADER: Say it again!

NEVILLE: No.

RINGLEADER: I said say it again!

NEVILLE: No.

[*The* RINGLEADER *gives his bird-call as a signal and the whole gang immediately attack* DANNY *and* NEVILLE. *A violent melée of arms, legs, punches — punctuated throughout with piercing bird-call war-cries.*]

35. Int. Mrs Graham's lounge. Teatime.

[MR *and* MRS GRAHAM *are seated at the table, ready to begin their meal.*

DANNY *and* NEVILLE — *with the odd cut, bruise and sticking plaster on their faces, are standing at the table, in their normal places for eating, except that, this time, nothing has been laid out for them.*]

MR GRAHAM [*head lowered*]: For what we're about to receive, may the Lord make us truly thankful.

    [DANNY *and* NEVILLE *look at their empty plates.*]

Amen.

MRS GRAHAM: Amen.

    [*She and* MR GRAHAM *begin eating. The boys just stand there.*]

Little boys who won't learn that fighting is wrong, get no tea.

    [*The* GRAHAMS *continue eating.*]

DANNY: Not even a pork sausage, Mrs Graham?

MRS GRAHAM: Were you given permission to speak?

DANNY [*thinks for a moment*]: Oh, no.

    [*They stand there in silence, apart from the clatter of* MR *and* MRS GRAHAM'*s knives and forks.*]

36. Int. The boys' bedroom. Evening.

[*The same evening.*

DANNY, *wearing pyjamas and schoolcap, is standing by the wall, re-positioning small swastikas and union jacks on a wall-map of France.*

NEVILLE *is in bed reading a comic.*

From downstairs we hear the muted sounds of ITMA on the wireless (or 'South of the Border'.]

DANNY: Why is it always *us* withdrawing and not the Germans?

    [NEVILLE *is preoccupied throughout the whole scene with his comic.*]

NEVILLE: To fortify positions or summat.

DANNY: Is that good?

NEVILLE: Yes. [*Pronounced* '*Yis*'.]

DANNY: It's 'Yes' not 'Yis'!

NEVILLE: No, it isn't.

DANNY: That's why they battered us!

NEVILLE: No, it wasn't.

[DANNY *looks at him, puzzled.*]

DANNY: I thought it *was*...?

NEVILLE: It was because they're Nazis.

DANNY: Who?

NEVILLE: Them kids. Just because we're not in their gang.

[DANNY *gets into bed and curls up, with his back to* NEVILLE.

Silence for a moment, apart from the wireless downstairs.]

DANNY: I'm going to tell my Mam about Mrs Graham.

[NEVILLE *looks up for the first time from his comic.*]

NEVILLE: You're bloomin' well *not*, our kid!

DANNY: I am!

NEVILLE: I'll belt you! She's got enough to worry about. You tell her nothing O.K.? Except we're dead happy.

[DANNY *lies there, his eyes open, staring miserably into space.* NEVILLE *relents a little.*]

Hey, our kid. Look.

[*He shows* DANNY *a 1940 pin-up of a girl in a bathing costume which has been torn from a magazine – and which he'd been looking at the whole time, hidden between the pages of his comic.*

DANNY *looks at it, unimpressed, not at all sure why he's been invited to look at it.*]

DANNY: It's a lady in a bathing costume.

NEVILLE [*smirking*]: I know.

DANNY: What about her?

NEVILLE [*grinning*]: You know...

DANNY: What?

NEVILLE [*giving up*]: Nothing. Go to sleep...

[*They try to settle down to sleep, both very hungry.*]

DANNY: Neville? Say for instance someone had no tea. How long would it be before they died?

NEVILLE: Go to sleep.

DANNY: If they got no breakfast either, they might be skeletons by school-time.

NEVILLE: There's a war on. You have to tighten your belt.

DANNY: I can't. My pyjama elastic's broke.

[*We hear* MRS GRAHAM *O.O.V., walking up the stairs.*

NEVILLE *quickly yanks* DANNY'*s cap off.*]

NEVILLE: Hey up! She's coming!

[DANNY *grabs his cap back and puts it on again. They both lie back feigning sleep.*

The footsteps get nearer.

At the last possible moment, DANNY *pulls his cap off and holds it under the bedclothes.*

MRS GRAHAM *pops her head into the room, peers first at one then the other, and satisfied they're asleep, switches the light off and exits, to return downstairs.*

DANNY *lies there in semi-darkness.*]

DANNY [*to himself*]: Blessed art Thou, O Lord our God, King of the Universe. Look after Mam and Dad and everyone, and let Hitler get cut up into little pieces with bayonets, and then burnt alive in boiling oil, then thrown in quicksand up to his neck while the ants eat him. And let him die slowly with toothache and horrible gashes. [*Pause.*] And the same goes for Mrs Graham. Only double.

37. Int. Mrs Graham's lounge.
(Continuous in time.)

[MRS GRAHAM *enters and starts tidying the room.*

MR GRAHAM *is sitting reading the evening paper. The radio music audible in the previous scene continues.*

MRS GRAHAM *picks up* DANNY'*s jacket from behind a chair to hang it up, when suddenly she holds it to her face and strokes it tenderly against her cheek. Guiltily she glances at* MR GRAHAM *to see if he saw her. He did, but quickly looks away. She briskly folds the jacket and continues tidying up. She glances back at her husband but he's now reading again.*]

38. Ext. street 'C', Cheetham Hill.

[*A queue of Jewish women are standing gossiping outside a grocery shop. The queue is hardly moving at all into the shop.*
GRANDMA *approaches, sees the queue, and decides to join it.*
Caption: 'May 19th 1940'.
GRANDMA *stands behind the last woman in the queue and exchanges a smile of recognition with her.*]

GRANDMA: So what are we queueing for?

WOMAN IN QUEUE: About three hours by the looks of it, believe me!

GRANDMA: Nu? How's the family, please God?

WOMAN IN QUEUE [*an enigmatic shrug*]: Ah.

GRANDMA [*enigmatic nods of the head*]: Mmmm.

WOMAN IN QUEUE: Yours?

GRANDMA: The same. [*Pause.*] And Yankel? He's enjoying jumping the parachutes?

WOMAN IN QUEUE [*proudly*]: A lance-corporal now, conohorry!

GRANDMA: That's good.

WOMAN IN QUEUE: Like Works Manager.

GRANDMA [*pleased*]: Mazeltov!

WOMAN IN QUEUE: And little Danny and Neville?

GRANDMA: Thank God. [*Meaning 'all right'.*]

WOMAN IN QUEUE: Thank God. [*Meaning 'thank God'.*]

GRANDMA: Today they have their Mamma. Every month she's there like a calendar. [*Sighs.*] Nine months now, already – who's counting . . .?

39. Ext. Blackpool pier. Day.

[*Open on an extremely pregnant girl sitting on a bench facing the sea. She's the girl from the sand-dunes (in Scene 33). She's knitting baby clothes.*
Track back to see that she's the first of a long line of women – all seated on benches, all knitting and all very pregnant.
SARAH, DANNY *and* NEVILLE (SARAH *hand-in-hand with each of them) are walking along from the prom towards the pregnant women.*
DANNY *and* NEVILLE *are wearing their balaclavas, now well worn.*
SARAH *is singing a favourite song of theirs, trying to jolly them up.*
NEVILLE *joins in now and then where he remembers the words.*
DANNY *isn't in the mood.*]

SARAH/NEVILLE [*singing*]:
>   Cheese and bread,
>   The old cow's head,
>   Roasted in a lantern,
>   A bit for you,
>   And a bit for me,
>   And a bit for Molly Dancers!
>   Cross-a-Molly,
>   Cross-a-Molly,
>   Cross-a-Molly Dancers!

[*As they pass by the pregnant women,* DANNY *stares at them, absolutely intrigued.*]

DANNY: Is it a knitting contest?
SARAH: Ssssh. Don't stare. Not nice.
DANNY: They've all got fat bellies.
NEVILLE: They're all pregnant.
DANNY: What's 'pregnant'?
SARAH [*staring at* NEVILLE]: Where did you hear that word?

NEVILLE: Sidney Zuckerman. It's not swearing. 'Nackers' is swearing.

SARAH [*shocked*]: Do you know what that *means*?

NEVILLE [*nonchalantly*]: It doesn't mean nothing. It's just swearing.

SARAH [*relaxing again*]: Oh, I see.

DANNY: What's 'pregnant'?

SARAH: They're having babies.

DANNY [*craning his head round to look at them*]: What – now?

SARAH: Soon. They've come here so's the babies won't get bombed.

[*They walk on.*]

DANNY: I thought they might've been spies.

NEVILLE: He thinks *everyone's* spies.

SARAH [*stopping*]: Hey! you two!

[*They stop and look at her. She takes a greaseproof paper parcel from her shopping bag.*]

Salt beef sandwich or Buzz Bar?

[*The boys leap in delight.*]

DANNY: High-ho, Silver!

NEVILLE: Both!!

40. Ext. Blackpool pier. A little later.

[DANNY *and* NEVILLE *are munching away at their sandwiches.*]

DANNY: Anyway – any German spy could stick a pillow up his jumper and sit there pretending he's pregnant.

NEVILLE: Shurrup, our kid. He gets on your nerves.

[SARAH *watches them a moment as they eat with enormous gusto.*]

SARAH: And are you still happy with Mrs Graham?

NEVILLE [*promptly*]: Yes.

SARAH: No complaints?

NEVILLE: No.

SARAH: And you still don't get homesick?

NEVILLE: No.

SARAH: Danny?

NEVILLE [*before* DANNY *can open his mouth*]: He doesn't either.

41. Ext. Photographer's stall on the pier.
An hour or so later.

[SARAH, DANNY *and* NEVILLE *stand with only their faces visible poking through the cut-outs in a huge 'comic scene' canvas. All three are laughing and giggling.*
The PHOTOGRAPHER *is preparing to take the picture.*]

PHOTOGRAPHER [*good-humouredly*]: Now settle down, you three! We haven't got all day.

[DANNY *immediately becomes conscious of the time and stops laughing.*
SARAH *realizes the reason for his sudden sadness.*]

DANNY: What time is it?

[SARAH *smiles at him, understandingly.*]

SARAH: I don't go back for *hours* yet . . .

DANNY: No one said you do. It's irrelevant.

42. Int. The Millers' living room. Evening.

[GRANDMA *is in her chair dozing – mouth wide open.*
From the wireless comes the voice of WINSTON CHURCHILL.]

CHURCHILL [*V.O.*]: 'I speak to you for the first time as Prime Minister in a solemn hour for the life of our country, of our Empire, of our Allies, and, above all, of the cause of Freedom . . .'

43. Ext. Street 'B', Cheetham Hill.
A few minutes later.

[LOUIS *is walking down the street towards his house. He carries a length of wood cut out into the shape of a rifle. The wireless of each house is tuned to Churchill, so that, as* LOUIS *passes the houses, we hear Churchill's speech continuing – its volume rising and falling with each house.*]

CHURCHILL [*V.O.*]: '. . . Behind them – behind us – behind the armies and fleets of Britain and France – gather a group of shattered States and bludgeoned races . . .'
    [LOUIS *passes* WILHELM, *who is against his wall, playing with a yo-yo or whip and top.* LOUIS *winks at him.*]
'. . . the Czechs, the Poles, the Norwegians, the Danes, the Dutch, the Belgians – upon all of whom the long night of barbarism will descend, unbroken even by a star of hope, unless we conquer, as conquer we must; as conquer we shall . . .'
    [LOUIS *turns into his own doorway.*]

44. Int. The Millers' living room.
(Continuous in time.)

[GRANDMA *wakes up on hearing the front door bang.*
LOUIS *enters. He's still carrying the rifle-shaped piece of wood. Churchill's speech continuous on the wireless.*]

CHURCHILL [*V.O.*]: '. . . Today is Trinity Sunday. Centuries ago words were written, to be a call and a spur to the faithful servants of Truth and Justice; Arm yourselves . . .'
    [GRANDMA *sees the ' gun'* LOUIS *is holding and screams.*]
'. . . and be ye men of valour, and be in readiness for the conflict . . .!'

LOUIS: It's not real!

GRANDMA: Oy libbergott!

LOUIS: It's a piece of wood! That's all we get in the L.D.V.s.

GRANDMA [*unconvinced*]: I know! I know! Just don't point, it's rude. Anyway, it might go off.

CHURCHILL [*V.O.*]: '. . . As the will of God is in Heaven, even so let it be.'

45. Int. Mrs Graham's lounge.
(Continuous in time.)

[MRS GRAHAM *is helping* SARAH *into her coat.* SARAH'*s case and shopping bag are at her feet – ready packed for her journey home.*]

MRS GRAHAM: There we are, dear.

SARAH: Thank you.

[DANNY *and* NEVILLE *are sitting side by side on the settee watching their mother with sinking hearts.*]

DANNY: Can we come to the station, Mam?

NEVILLE: To see you off, Mam?

MRS GRAHAM [*before* SARAH *can reply*]: Oh, it's much too late for little boys to be out, isn't it, Mrs Miller, of course it is.

[SARAH *stands, ready but reluctant to go.*]

SARAH: Well . . . I'll . . . I'll love you and leave you. Thanks for putting me up again, Mrs Graham.

MRS GRAHAM: Our pleasure, wasn't it, children?

[SARAH *stands there – the boys watching her.*]

It's a shame you can't stay a little longer, really . . .

SARAH: Yes. [*To the boys*] I'll be back next month. We'll have fun *again*.

MRS GRAHAM [*laughing indulgently*]: Oh, they never stop, them two! My husband terms them Jewell and Warriss, after the comedians.

[SARAH *smiles at the boys.*]

SARAH: I'll say ta, ra, then.

> [DANNY and NEVILLE stand up.
>
> SARAH glances at MRS GRAHAM to see if she intends to leave them in private to say their farewells. MRS GRAHAM stays firmly put, smiling politely. SARAH resigns herself to it. She kisses the two boys.]

Danny. Neville.

DANNY: }
NEVILLE: } Ta, ra, Mam.

SARAH: Be good boys now. See you very, very soon. Pip, pip, pip.

> [She picks up her shopping bag and small case and exits with MRS GRAHAM following her out.
>
> The two boys stand there. DANNY takes his Dinky Toy racing car from his pocket quietly, vrumm-vrumms it on the table for a moment, then puts it back in his pocket.
>
> We hear MRS GRAHAM and SARAH bidding each other goodbye at the door. The door bangs to.
>
> MRS GRAHAM re-enters and starts busying herself tidying up.]

MRS GRAHAM [briskly, businesslike]: Isn't she nice? Lovely hair, hasn't she?

DANNY [with quiet pride]: She dyes it. She's a peroxide blonde. I used to watch her doing the roots.

46. Ext. Blackpool street. Evening.

[SARAH walks down the street, away from the house. She's very close to tears.]

47. Int. Boys' bedroom. Later the same night.

[DANNY is re-positioning swastikas on his wall-map ... The Union Jacks continuing their retreat towards Dunkirk.

NEVILLE, in his pyjamas, is about to get into bed. He stops at the *dressing-table and takes his comic from his satchel. He opens it and starts to take from it his pin-up, which is hidden between the pages. He changes his mind, puts the pin-up back into the comic, and the comic back into his satchel. He slings the satchel onto the floor and climbs into bed.*

From downstairs we can hear the wireless play the opening signature tune of 'The Happidrome'.

DANNY *gets into bed. For the first time, it's* NEVILLE *who quietly starts to cry.* DANNY *turns – and is about to start crying himself. Instead he bites his lip – and belts* NEVILLE *across the head.*]

48. Ext. Bicycle shed, school playground. Day.

[*From inside a nearby classroom, we hear a class of boys chanting in unison 'Cargoes' by John Masefield.*

ZUCKERMAN *appears, creeping surreptitiously from the back of the shed. Bundled in his arms are his cap, coat, haversack, gas-mask case and paper parcel. From the parcel he takes a pair of roller-skates and starts putting them on, keeping a wary look-out as he does so.*]

49. Ext. Another part of school playground.

[NEVILLE's *class are playing football, dressed in their normal school clothes.* NEVILLE *is in goal. The 'goalposts' are bundles of jackets put down by the boys. While play is at the other end* NEVILLE *is standing on his own. He suddenly picks up one of the 'goalposts' – which is composed of his own cap, coat, haversack, and gas-mask case – and dashes off with them, towards the bicycle shed.*]

50. Ext. Boys' toilets, playground.

[DANNY *emerges surreptitiously from the toilets, carrying his clothes and haversack, etc. He walks along with an innocent nonchalance for a few yards, then suddenly makes a frantic dash towards the bicycle shed.*]

51. Ext. Bicycle shed, school playground.

[ZUCKERMAN *is now fully dressed, his haversack on his back, and is fastening his roller-skates on.*
NEVILLE *is beside him – also fully dressed. He takes a pair of roller-skates from his coat pockets and starts fastening one of them on.*
DANNY *arrives, struggling hurriedly into his coat and haversack.*
NEVILLE *passes him his other skate.* DANNY *starts putting it on. They speak conspiratorially.*]

ZUCKERMAN: Did you ask to leave the room?
DANNY: Yes.
ZUCKERMAN [*alarmed*]: To wee? That's what *I* said!
DANNY: No, a bilious attack.

    [ZUCKERMAN *watches the others fastening on their single skates.*]
    Do you think you'll be O.K. with just one each?
NEVILLE: Prisoners of war don't even have *none* even!

    [*They continue getting ready, with* ZUCKERMAN – *just a little scared – keeping look-out.*]
ZUCKERMAN: Ready?
NEVILLE: Hang on a sec!
ZUCKERMAN: Say Roger and Out when you are.
DANNY: How will we know the way – with all the signposts blacked out?
ZUCKERMAN: I've got a compass.
NEVILLE: And a map?
ZUCKERMAN: I can't follow maps.

NEVILLE [*incredulously*]: Well, what good's a – you're barmy aren't you! What are you?

ZUCKERMAN: We'll ask people the way. Not coppers, though. Or we'll be nackered. Ready?

DANNY: Yes.

NEVILLE: Yes.

ZUCKERMAN: Say Roger and Out.

DANNY/NEVILLE: Roger and Out.

[*Stealthily they skate out of the school-yard and into the street –* DANNY *and* NEVILLE *running on one foot and skating on the other.*]

52. Ext. Blackpool, street 'D'.

[*The three of them are skating along. They pass a newsagent's placard:* ' *B.E.F. evacuates Dunkirk'.*]

53. Ext. Blackpool, street 'E'.

[*The three of them are skating along.*]

54. Ext. Blackpool promenade.

[ZUCKERMAN *and* NEVILLE *skating along.* ZUCKERMAN *is wearing his gas-mask.*
DANNY *is falling further and further behind and appears to be in trouble. Suddenly his skate collapses. He stops.*]

DANNY [*calling*]: Our kid!!

[NEVILLE *and* ZUCKERMAN *stop and turn.*]

NEVILLE: Trust you! Orky Duck . . .

[NEVILLE *and* ZUCKERMAN *skate back to* DANNY, *who shows them his skate. Two of the wheels have broken off.*]

DANNY: Are we nearly there?

ZUCKERMAN: We're not even in Preston yet.

> [*A pause. Nobody knows what to do.*
>
> ZUCKERMAN *takes off his gas-mask.*]

Have you got the busfare back?

NEVILLE: I've got a shilling.

DANNY: You two go on . . .

NEVILLE: No. Zuckie can. I'll come back with you.

DANNY: No, Nev! It's your big chance.

NEVILLE: No. She'd only put you in solitary confinement.

> [*He starts taking his skate off.*
>
> *The others watch unhappily.*]

DANNY: Can we *walk* it to Manchester!!

NEVILLE [*shaking his head*]: Too far.

ZUCKERMAN [*sympathetically*]: Best go back, Danny.

> [DANNY *nods sadly. An uncomfortable silence.*]

ZUCKERMAN: Ta, ra, men.

NEVILLE: See you after the duration, Zuckie.

ZUCKERMAN: If I collect any shrapnel, I'll save you some.

> [*He hitches up his haversack, puts his gas-mask on again and skates off on his way.*
>
> DANNY *and* NEVILLE, *fed up, frustrated, start off back to Blackpool.* NEVILLE *gives* DANNY *a dirty look – which* DANNY *notices.*]

DANNY [*tearfully*]: It wasn't *my* fault!!

> [NEVILLE *launches into him, fists flying; they fight and wrestle for a few moments.* NEVILLE *gets* DANNY *to the ground and straddles over him, then suddenly stops – struck by a sudden thought.*
>
> DANNY *looks up from his vanquished position.*]

Do you give in?

NEVILLE [*half to himself*]: He could've given you one of his!!

DANNY: What?

NEVILLE [*getting up*]: We could've had one skate each! [*He shouts down the road.*] Zuckie! Zuckie! Wait!

> [*In vain . . .* ZUCKERMAN *is out of sight.*

NEVILLE *shrugs.*] [*sighing*] Come on. Deadly Night-
shade.

[*He starts tramping off back towards Blackpool.*
DANNY *gets up and trudges after him.*]

55. Int. The Millers' cellar. Night.

[*The furniture is composed of boxes and blankets. To one side is an
area piled high with coal.*
SARAH *is knitting. The sounds of an air-raid are not too distant.*
GRANDMA *enters, wearing a pinny and carrying a saucepan of
soup and a soup-ladle.*]

GRANDMA: Who wants some nice chicken soup, yes? Ask
a meshugganah question – everybody!

[SARAH *mutters* 'no, thanks.'
GRANDMA *waits a moment, then tries again.*]

[*Temptingly*] Warms the kichkes, nice . . .

[*She smacks her lips. Again,* SARAH *declines her offer.*]

Nice drop of chicken soup for the air-raid. Special recom-
mended.

[*Again,* SARAH *refuses.*]

Do you good when the bombs drop. The King and Queen
have it.

SARAH: How can chicken soup do you good if you're blown
to smithereens?

GRANDMA: God forbid! [*She spits three times.*]

SARAH: Wouldn't do you any good *then* would it?

GRANDMA [*shrugs*]: It wouldn't do you any *harm* . . .

[GRANDMA *turns to exit back upstairs, as* LOUIS *enters,
putting on his cap and coat and carrying a torch.*]

[*To* LOUIS] A meshugganah missus you've got. [*She exits.*]

LOUIS: See you later.

SARAH: I thought Bernard was fire-watching tonight?

LOUIS: So, I'll *help* him, terrible thing! Ta, ra.

[*She calls* 'Ta ra' *after him as he exits.*

The sounds of the air-raid become nearer and heavier.
GRANDMA *re-enters, carrying a saucepan.*]
SARAH: You won't take no for an answer, will you!
GRANDMA [*sitting on a box*]: It's a different pan, what you
talk? This one's milkadicky.
[*She inverts it and puts it on her head as a helmet.*
SARAH *laughs.*]
Nu? Someone told you a good joke? Issy Bonn, maybe?
Laugh – gezuntereit!

56. Ext. Factory. Night.

[*Smoking debris and rubble.*
The scream and exploding roar of bombs.
Shouts, whistles, burning wood.
Perhaps an ambulance and fire engine.]

57. Int. Factory. Night.

[*Smoke, debris. Outside, bombs are falling and buildings burning.*
LOUIS, *together with* BERNARD (*another firewatching employee*)
and a FIREMAN, *is standing over a corpse, which is half covered by a*
blanket. LOUIS *and* BERNARD *are coming to the end of 'Yitgadal'*
– the Hebrew prayer of mourning. They're wearing their caps: the
FIREMAN *holds his helmet in his hands.*
A ST JOHN AMBULANCE MAN *clambers in, sees the corpse.*]

AMBULANCE MAN: He's the only one, is he?
FIREMAN: Incendiary in the yard. He came rushing in . . .
Got half the roof on his head . . .
[*The* AMBULANCE MAN *bends over the body. The corpse*
is MERTON – *the budding footballer from Scene 5.*]
AMBULANCE MAN: Bit of a kid . . .
FIREMAN: Used to run messages for us on his bike . . .
Marvellous footballer, I believe.

AMBULANCEMAN [*getting up*]: Not any more . . .

FIREMAN: No. Seventeen. Breaks your heart.

LOUIS: Fifteen.

FIREMAN [*puzzled*]: You have to be seventeen before you
can . . .

LOUIS: Honest. He was a pal of my two lads. I'd best go
and tell his Mam.

58. Ext. Blackpool Station.

[DANNY *and* NEVILLE *standing waiting to meet* SARAH *off the
train. The train pulls in. Passengers – mostly servicemen and women
– get out.* DANNY *and* NEVILLE *look, with growing anxiety, up
and down the quickly emptying platform.
A* SAILOR *gets out.*]

NEVILLE: Mister!

SAILOR: The Navy don't have capbadges. Ask a soldier.

NEVILLE: No . . . just is this the train from Manchester?

SAILOR: Yes.

DANNY: Are you sure?

NEVILLE: Thank you.

> [*The* SAILOR *walks off.*
> DANNY *calls after him.*]

DANNY: Are you positive?

> [*The* SAILOR *ignores him.*
> DANNY *and* NEVILLE *stand peering disconsolately down the
> platform. No one else gets off. They're left alone.*]

NEVILLE: Come on.

DANNY: Why hasn't she come?

NEVILLE: Stop shlurrying your feet.

> [*He prods* DANNY *towards the barrier.
> As they go, sadly, we hear* SARAH, *voice over.*]

SARAH [*V.O.*]: 'Dear Neville and Danny, Just a quick line
to let you know all is well at this end. I'm sorry I couldn't
come on Saturday as promised, only your Dad's been off

work a few days owing to an accidental fire at the factory. Someone must have dropped a cigarette-end or something. So to get some extra pennies and get the war over quicker, I've stayed to do some overtime. I hope you didn't mind, and I'll definitely be over before you can say Jack Robinson. Everyone sends their regards. All your pals and everyone is very well, so there's nothing to worry about, is there? Be good boys to Mr and Mrs Graham. Lots of Love. Pip, pip, pip. Your loving Mam and Dad.'

(Scenes 59 to 64 are a montage sequence.
Musical link – early war pop-song.)

59. Ext. Grocery shop, Street 'C', Cheetham Hill.

[*The broken shop-window is boarded up with planks across which is a painted: 'Business as usual'.*
GRANDMA *walks into the shop, carrying her purse and shopping basket.*]

60. Int. Grocery shop.

[*The shopkeeper,* MR GROSSFINE, *is giving* GRANDMA *one egg.*]

GRANDMA: So what's this, Mr Grossfine?
MR GROSSFINE: This week's ration, Mrs Miller.
GRANDMA: Very nice. Monday I'll bake with it. Tuesday I'll chop herrings with it. Wednesday I'll fry it. Thursday I'll boil it. Friday, with a bit of mazel, I'll sit on it, and hatch chickens of my own . . .
MR GROSSFINE [*shrugs*]: Mrs Miller. Is it my fault?
GRANDMA [*firmly*]: Mr Grossfine, I want a dozen. [*Ingratiatingly*] I knew your father, ovoshalom. With no tochass in his hazen.
MR GROSSFINE [*wearily*]: Pass me your ration book. I'll explain.

[GRANDMA *hands him her identity card from her shopping bag.*]

That's your identity card. I want your ration book.

GRANDMA: Blackshirt! [*She raps his knuckles.*] Nah!

61. Int. Munitions factory.

[SARAH *is working with two or three more women at a bench. They wear goggles and use welding equipment. They're singing an early war pop-song in accompaniment with a vocalist on the wireless.*

A MAN IN OVERALLS *passes, carrying a crate labelled 'W/D bullets 837/9'.*]

MAN IN OVERALLS: Here you are, Sarah. For your Louis. [*He takes a cigarette-lighter, made in the shape of a bullet, from the crate, flicks it alight to test it, and gives it to her*].

SARAH: I thought we were making *bullets*?

MAN IN OVERALLS: Ssshh. Careless talk costs lives. Have another. [*He hands her another lighter.*]

62. Ext. Synagogue, Cheetham Hill.

[*From inside, we hear the chanting of Hebrew prayers. One of the windows is broken. Over it is a piece of cardboard on which is painted: 'Business as usual'.*]

63. Int. Synagogue.

[*Two men, wearing yarmulka or hat, and tallis (long shawl), are chanting Hebrew devoutly from their prayer-books. (More voices off, chanting in unison.) Still chanting, the first man takes from his raincoat pocket a bag of Tate and Lyle sugar and hands it, without looking, to the second man. He, in turn, takes from his pocket a paper bag. The first man takes it, opens it to reveal a piece of raw*

steak, nods. closes it again. Both men pocket their exchanged goods,
and devoutly continue praying.]

64. Ext. Street 'B', Cheetham Hill.

[*A woman is rushing down the street, knocking on each door, then
opening each door and calling inside – 'Mrs Levi! Bananas at the
Co-op!' 'Mrs Abrams! Bananas at the Co-op!' 'Mrs Miller . . .'.*
[SARAH *emerges from her front door, struggling into her coat.*]

SARAH: I heard! I heard!
    [*She,* MRS LEVI *and* MRS ABRAMS *dash out of their houses
    and race off down the street towards the Co-op. The woman
    continues knocking at each door and calling the good news.*]

65. Int. Mrs Graham's lounge. Evening.

[*Open on* DANNY *and* NEVILLE *eating bananas. They're sitting
round the fire with* MRS GRAHAM *and* SARAH *– who is on the
latest of her visits.*
In evidence are one or two games – Ludo, snakes and ladders, etc.
It's late Sunday afternoon – an hour or so before SARAH *is due to
catch her train home again. Consequently,* DANNY *and* NEVILLE
are in fairly subdued moods.]

SARAH: Another game, kids?
DANNY: You haven't time. Your train goes in –
SARAH: How about 'I spy'?
MRS GRAHAM: I think they're probably a little overtired . . .
SARAH [*thinking of a game*]: I know! 'Silly Story'!
NEVILLE: What's that?
SARAH: You get a piece of paper and everyone writes down
  a –
DANNY: I can't play it.
MRS GRAHAM: You don't know what it is yet, child!

[*She smooths his hair down maternally.* SARAH *notices –
but pretends that she hasn't.*]

SARAH [*to the boys*]: I write the beginning of a story – something silly – and fold the paper over so's the next one can't
read it. Then he writes *his* daft sentence, and folds it over
and passes it to the next and –

DANNY: It's silly.

NEVILLE: That's the idea, barm-pot.

SARAH: And when we've all finished, we read the whole
thing out, and it makes a Silly Story – and we all laugh!

MRS GRAHAM [*to the boys*]: I'll show you.

[MRS GRAHAM *takes pencil and paper and starts writing,
laughing to herself at her story.*

DANNY *sits watching solemnly and ignores* SARAH'*s re-
assuring smile.*

MRS GRAHAM *folds the paper and passes it to* NEVILLE,
who starts writing.]

DANNY: I won't know what to put . . .

SARAH: Whatever comes into your head.

[*An idea is slowly forming in* DANNY'*s mind. He seems
scared – and a little excited . . .*

NEVILLE, *grinning at what he's written, folds the paper and
hands it to* DANNY.

DANNY *looks at each of them tensely.*]

MRS GRAHAM: You put whatever you *want*, child!

[DANNY *reaches his decision. He starts writing thoughtfully.
The others watch him – amused at his concentration.*]

Come on, slowcoach!

[DANNY *continues writing, tongue stuck out in concentration.*]

NEVILLE [*impatiently*]: Oh, blimey!

[DANNY *finally folds the paper and hands it to* SARAH. *She
starts writing, smiling at her story.* DANNY *sits nervously
looking from one to the other.*]

DANNY: Read it.

SARAH: In a minute. [*She finishes writing and unfolds the
paper.*] Right. [*Reading*] 'Once upon a time, there were
two princes called Danny and Neville who lived in a

Castle called Blackpool Tower, with the other monkeys!'

[SARAH *smiles at* MRS GRAHAM, *who smiles back, proud of her story.* SARAH *unfolds the paper further and continues with* NEVILLE's *contribution.*]

[*Reading*] '... And then the Spitfires attacked the Messerschmitt, and the German pilot shouted "Get off my foot!"'

[*She,* NEVILLE, *and* MRS GRAHAM *laugh.*
DANNY *watches the paper in* SARAH's *hands, tensely.*
SARAH *unfolds it again and starts to read* DANNY's *contribution.*]

[*Reading*] 'She is dead cruel to us. She steals your letters and ...

[SARAH *stops and looks at* DANNY. *He sits impassively.*
MRS GRAHAM *stares from one to the other, blankly.*
SARAH *slowly resumes reading, aloud* ...]

'She is dead cruel to us. She steals your letters ... and whatever you send us. She makes us clean and polish the house every day, and gives us rotten dinners. She hates us. And we hate her back. All this is secret. We want to come home.'

[*She lowers the paper onto her lap.*
Everyone seems frozen to stone – except SARAH.]

[*Quietly, calmly*] Is this true, Danny?

DANNY [*quietly*]: Yes, Mam.

SARAH: Emess?

DANNY: Emess adashem.

SARAH [*turning to* NEVILLE]: Neville?

NEVILLE [*nodding, scared*]: Yes, Mam.

[SARAH *turns to* MRS GRAHAM.]

SARAH: Mrs Graham?

66. Int. The Millers' living room. Evening.

[*It's the first night of 'Chanuka' – the Jewish Festival of the Lights. The eight-stemmed candelabra is in the centre of the table.*]

LOUIS *is seated at the table, wearing his yarmulka, sorting out the prayer books, ready to start the informal, family service.*

DANNY, NEVILLE *and* SARAH, *led by* GRANDMA, *who holds aloft a lighted candle – are doing a wild conga round the room. They're singing, as follows.*]

ALL: 'Mo outsur y'shuosee / L'cho noeh / L'shabeyach / Teecoun base t'filosee / V'shom toudoh / N'zabeyach ... Mo outsur Y'shuosee – [*Then even more loudly*] the cat's in the cupboard and he can't see me!!!

LOUIS: Yes, all right. Can we get started now?

    [GRANDMA *lights the first candle with the one she's holding, then places it into the centre holder.*]

    [*To the boys*] Now you know why we're doing this, don't you?

DANNY: 'Cos we haven't got a shilling for the meter!

NEVILLE [*parrot-fashion*]: The festival of Chanuka is to commemorate the return of the Israelites to the Temple, after forty years in the wilderness. In the Temple there was –

DANNY: Dad asked *me*!!

NEVILLE [*ignoring him*]: ... there was only enough oil in the lamp to last for one day, but –

DANNY: Mam, stop him!

NEVILLE: ... But God worked a miracle –

DANNY: Anybody knows that!

NEVILLE: ... and it burned for eight days instead.

DANNY [*hastily to* LOUIS]: So we light a candle each night for eight nights, till they're all lit! Amen. [*He pulls his tongue at* NEVILLE.] Clever-dick!

    [*The sirens begin to sound.*
    They all fall silent.
    SARAH *looks at the clock.*]

SARAH: Ten minutes early tonight.

67. Int. The boys' bedroom (Blackpool).
Evening.

[*The room looks sparse and bare. All the boys' belongings have gone
– including* DANNY's *wall map.*
*There's a sudden, heavy silence in contrast to the noise of the
previous scene.*
MRS GRAHAM, *her eyes empty, is stripping the beds down to their
mattresses.*
MR GRAHAM, *evening paper in his hand, appears at the door. He
smiles briefly, stiffly, at her, in an awkward attempt at cheeriness.*]

MRS GRAHAM [*quietly, evenly*]: He tells lies, young Danny, I
didn't hate them.

MR GRAHAM: 'Course not . . .

MRS GRAHAM: I taught them respect, yes. Agreed. To
respect their elders and betters. I wouldn't say that was
cruel.

MR GRAHAM: Only way really . . .

MRS GRAHAM: I'd say that was love. That's the word I'd
give it. [*Pause.*] Her love isn't love at all. Too *much* love . . .
[*A pause.*]

MR GRAHAM: Not to worry . . .

MRS GRAHAM: No. [*She works silently for a moment.*] *That's*
what's cruel. [*She looks at him.*] I asked her to let me adopt
them . . . officially . . .

MR GRAHAM: Come downstairs, love . . .

MRS GRAHAM [*fighting the tears*]: I had to make them try and
forget her, Gordon, hadn't I?
[*He looks at her uneasily.*]

MR GRAHAM: Their own *mother*?

MRS GRAHAM: *I* was their mother!
[*A silence. They stand looking helplessly at each other.*]

MR GRAHAM [*going to her*]: Come on, love.
[*She allows herself to be led to the door, his arm round her
shoulder.*]

Atta girl . . .
 [*They exit.*]

68. Int. The Millers' cellar. Night.

[*Aircraft flying in waves overhead. Bombs screaming nearby.*
DANNY, NEVILLE, SARAH *and* GRANDMA *are now all sitting
with saucepans on their heads – and all a little nerve-wracked.*]

NEVILLE [*addressing the German bombers*]: Hurry up, I'm
 tired. I want to gay schloffen.
DANNY [*abruptly*]: Don't you start, German sausage!
NEVILLE [*puzzled*]: What?
DANNY: Spouting German! It's bad enough with *her*!
 [*Meaning* GRANDMA.]
SARAH [*shocked*]: Danny!
NEVILLE [*defensively*]: It wasn't German. It was Yiddish.
DANNY: It's the same thing!
NEVILLE: It never is – is it, Mam?
GRANDMA [*puzzled*]: All the Yiddishe talk Yiddish – that's
 why they're Yiddishe . . .
DANNY: It's German!
GRANDMA [*shouting*]: So it's German. Does that makes it
 German?
DANNY [*almost crying in anger*]: It's the Germans who are
 bombing us!
 [*They sit there quietly. Disturbed.*
 The all clear begins to sound.
 They start gathering their things to return upstairs.]
GRANDMA: All of a sudden he's anti-semitic against the
 Jews . . .
 [NEVILLE *bursts into laughter.*
 GRANDMA *looks at him puzzled.*]
 Nu?
NEVILLE: You can't be anti-semitic against the Christians,
 can you!

[DANNY, *angrily silent ever since his outburst, exits upstairs.*
NEVILLE *watches him go.*]
What's got into the little rabbi?
SARAH: He's growing. I can tell by his clothes.

69. Int. The Millers' living room.

[*A little later the same night.*

DANNY, *in pyjamas, is re-lighting the principal candle in the
candelabra. He starts then lighting the remaining eight — which are
not too firmly stuck in their holders.*]

70. Int. Parents' bedroom.
(Continuous in time.)

[SARAH *is in bed.*
LOUIS *is undressing for bed.*]

LOUIS: Town was hit bad, I believe. Blackfriars . . . Cannon
Street. And Trafford Park got another pasting. The
docks . . .
SARAH [*calling*]: Danny, are you in bed yet?
DANNY [*O.O.V.*]: Nearly.
SARAH [*calling*]: What are you doing down there?

71. Int. The Millers' living room.
(Continuous in time.)

[DANNY *is gazing expressionlessly at the row of burning candles.*]
DANNY [*calling*]: Nowt. [*He exits.*]

72. Int. Parents' bedroom. A few minutes later.

[SARAH *and* LOUIS *are lying in bed.*]

LOUIS [*slightly troubled*]: Danny said a rum thing. When I told him about Merton being dead. I said his Mam and Dad were heartbroken . . . their only son being killed. He said, 'So what? They can always have another.'

73. Int. The boys' bedroom. (Continuous in time.)

[DANNY *and* NEVILLE *are lying in their beds.*]

NEVILLE: Goodnight, our kid.
DANNY: Goodnight.
   [NEVILLE *settles down to sleep, then suddenly starts up again.*]
NEVILLE: Hey! Can you smell burning?
DANNY: No?
   [*We hear the crackling of wood burning downstairs. The bedroom slowly fills with smoke.*]
Yes!!
   [*The boys leap out of bed.*]
NEVILLE: Dad!! [*He races to the door.*] Dad, the house is on fire!
   [*We hear doors banging, running feet, shouting.*
   DANNY *is sitting on the edge of his bed, struggling to get his socks on.*]
DANNY [*calling out*]: It must be a time-bomb. Delayed action.
LOUIS [*O.O.V.*]: Downstairs – all of you – quick!
SARAH [*O.O.V.*]: Danny, come on! Mother – never mind your teeth!
DANNY [*calling*]: It could be a Molotov Bread-basket. With delayed action.
   [SARAH *dashes in, in dressing-gown.*]

SARAH: Not the only one, is it? [*She drags him out, with one sock on.*]

74. Int. The Millers' living room. (Continuous in time.)

[LOUIS *is stamping on what's left of the curtains, which are in flames on the floor. There are smouldering burns on adjacent furniture, the ceiling and carpet. The tablecloth is burnt to ashes.*
SARAH, GRANDMA, NEVILLE *and* DANNY *are huddled together in the doorway watching* LOUIS *put out the fire.*
We hear A.R.P. whistles outside, and men's voices shouting.]

DANNY: Was it a Molotov Bread-Basket, Dad?
   [LOUIS *sighs, picks up the blackened candelabra and looks at him pointedly.*]
LOUIS: No, Danny. A bloody candle!
   [*We hear more A.R.P. whistles and, much to* DANNY'*s horror, a fire engine approaching with bells ringing.*
   The family all turn to look at DANNY *accusingly.*]
DANNY [*faintly*]: Oy, gevalt . . .

75. Int. Classroom. Day.

[*The room is empty apart from* ZUCKERMAN *and* DANNY.
It's some months later. DANNY *now wears* NEVILLE'*s old cast-offs, and* ZUCKERMAN *wears spectacles. They're taking out* MR GOLDSTONE'*s desk drawers and putting them back upside down.*
DANNY *is rummaging in his satchel. He gets out his Dinky Toy racing car, and places it beside a lump of shrapnel on his desk. He looks from one to the other, trying to evaluate their worth.*]

DANNY: Will you take this for it? [*He holds up the racing car.*]
ZUCKERMAN: What – for a real piece of landmine?
DANNY: Are you sure it's not just ack-ack shell?
ZUCKERMAN: Any money.

[*The door opens and* MR GOLDSTONE *enters with a ten-year-old boy, who's wearing cap, coat, gas-mask case round his shoulders, identification label, and carries a suitcase.*]

MR GOLDSTONE: You two know the bell's gone?

DANNY:
ZUCKERMAN: } Yes, Sir.

MR GOLDSTONE: Got no homes to go to?

DANNY:
ZUCKERMAN: } Yes. Sir.

DANNY: Please Sir, I'm just waiting for my brother from Standard Five.

ZUCKERMAN: Please Sir, I was helping the ink-monitor.

MR GOLDSTONE: Either of you live near Elizabeth Street?

DANNY:
ZUCKERMAN: } Yes, Sir.

MR GOLDSTONE: Good. [*He takes some papers from his desk and gives them to the small boy.*] Take this boy to Mrs Bloom, Number 110, Elizabeth Street. She's taking him in. He's an evacuee from London. Philip Hyman. Philip's just arrived. Say hello to each other.

DANNY:
ZUCKERMAN: } Hello.

PHILIP: Hello.

MR GOLDSTONE: See you in the morning, Hyman.

PHILIP; Yes, Sir.

[MR GOLDSTONE *exits.*]

DANNY: I used to be an evacuee when I was a kid.

PHILIP: So what?

[*He stands watching* DANNY *put his racing car back in his satchel and rummage for something else to swop.*

PHILIP *notices the bathing-beauty pin-up photo which* NEVILLE *had in Blackpool sticking out of the satchel; he takes it and looks at it — now very dog-eared and creased.*]

Who's this?

DANNY: No one! [*He grabs it back from* PHILIP *and stuffs it back into his satchel.*]

76. Ext. Street 'D', Cheetham Hill. Half an hour later.

[DANNY, NEVILLE, ZUCKERMAN *and* PHILIP, *carrying his suitcase, are walking towards Elizabeth Street.*
One or two other boys from school are some little distance behind them, walking home.
A little further behind is WILHELM, *walking home alone.*]

NEVILLE [*to* PHILIP]: What do you reckon to Manchester, then?
PHILIP [*very strong Cockney accent*]: S'all right. Can't grumble.
　　[DANNY *stops dead in his tracks and stares at him with amused incredulity.*]
DANNY [*mimicking*]: 'Grumble'??? 'Grumble'??? Got a right Cockney twang, hasn't he?
NEVILLE: Shrurrup, our kid. [*To* PHILIP] We get air-raids here an' all you know . . .
PHILIP: Not like us. We get *tons*. Every night.
　　[DANNY *is now hysterically beside himself at* PHILIP'*s accent.*]
DANNY [*mimicking*]: 'Tons'!!! Every 'night'!
　　[NEVILLE *and* ZUCKERMAN *find it difficult not to laugh.*]
　　[*to* PHILIP] It's 'tons' and 'night'. [*Both with Manchester pronunciation.*] Not 'tons' and 'night'. [*Cockney pronunciation.*]
PHILIP: No, it ain't.
DANNY: Say it again. Say 'grumble'.
PHILIP: I shan't.
DANNY: I said 'say it again'!
PHILIP: I heard you!
　　[DANNY *pins him against a wall. On it is chalked 'Open the second front now!'*]
DANNY: Say it again!
PHILIP: Bugger off!
　　[DANNY *promptly laces into him and punches him in the stomach.*

PHILIP *groans.*]

You rotten pig! I've just had my appendix out!

DANNY [*dropping his fists, then, sympathetically*]: Sorry.

[PHILIP *promptly punches* DANNY *in his unguarded mouth.*]

NEVILLE: Look, quit it, you two!

DANNY [*inarticulately*]: He's knocked a tooth loose!

NEVILLE [*grabbing his arm*]: Come on. [*He starts leading* DANNY *away.*]

DANNY [*inarticulately*]: Rotten Londoner ... [*He points to his teeth.*] Look. That one.

NEVILLE [*pushing him*]: Get home.

[WILHELM *has now drawn level with them.*]

[*to* WILHELM, *not expecting a reply*] Hi-de-hi.

WILHELM [*grinning*]: Ho-de-ho!

NEVILLE [*amazed*]: Hey, Danny! Hear that! He *spoke*! Wilhelm *spoke*!!

[DANNY *tries to tell* WILHELM *about his loose tooth – but the words are an incoherent mumble. He pulls his jaw open, to show the damage.*

WILHELM *smiles at him – and walks on alongside* NEVILLE, ZUCKERMAN *and* PHILIP. *They all talk among themselves.*

DANNY *trundles behind, holding his jaw, mumbling to himself. They walk on towards Elizabeth Street ... away from camera.*]

THE END

Spend, Spend, Spend

First transmission date 15 March 1977

Produced by Graeme McDonald
Directed by John Goldschmidt

VIVIAN NICHOLSON	Susan Littler
KEITH NICHOLSON	John Duttine
VIVIAN'S MOTHER	Helen Beck
VIVIAN'S FATHER	Joe Belcher
MATTHEW	Stephen Bill
KEITH'S GRANNY	Liz Smith
GIRLFRIEND	Annie Hulley
GARY	Philip Joseph
PUBLIC RELATIONS MAN	John Lyons
PUBLIC RELATIONS GIRL	Jane Lowe
TAXI DRIVER	Jack Platts
DOCTOR	Fred Gaunt
FIRST WOMAN	Joan Peters
SECOND WOMAN	Joyce Kennedy
FIRST POLICEMAN	Peter Russell
SECOND POLICEMAN	Gordon Wharmby
POSTMAN	Bert Oxley
MAN FROM THE POOLS	Robin Boncey

1. Int. A corridor at the Dorchester Hotel.
(September 1961.)

[*Open tight on* KEITH *and* VIVIAN: *Both of them stiffly and uncomfortably dressed in brand-new clothes.* VIVIAN's *hair is freshly coiffured – and dyed pink. They're both terrified and overawed and racked with nerves. They hold drinks in their hands – and they're more than a little tipsy.*
Standing just inside the open door is a PUBLIC RELATIONS GIRL, *clutching a clipboard of papers. She's keeping one wary eye on* KEITH *and* VIVIAN, *and the other on events in the main reception room on the other side of the door.*
From the main reception room, we hear the noise, bustle, chatter and laughter of a mob of reporters and photographers. As well as being here for the beer, they're also, somewhat excitedly, preparing to cover what they rightly suspect is to be the biggest pools story of the season.
From inside the reception room we hear a PUBLIC RELATIONS MAN *trying to bring them to order.*]

P.R. MAN [*O.O.V.*]: Right, thank you, gentlemen! Ladies and gentlemen! [*Louder*] Thank you! Thank you, everyone!
[*The hubbub begins to subside.*]
Sorry to rush you, but you do have a deadline to meet – [*laughs briefly*] at least, I *hope* you do, so if you're ready, I think *we* are...
[*The hubbub subsides a little more.*]
KEITH [*nervously*]: Christ, you look rough...
VIVIAN: I feel a bit sick.
KEITH: I'm not surprised. Rate you've been knocking them back.
VIVIAN [*without interest*]: You've spilt brandy on your fly.
[*Pause. They sit, trembling with nerves.*]
VIVIAN: Is my hair nice? Champagne blonde? It's all the go, champagne blonde. Pink were called pink when I

went to school. They call it champagne blonde down here. [*Pause. She fights back bile in her throat.*] I don't know whether to pass out or throw up . . .

    [*She immediately takes another gulp from her glass. The* P.R. GIRL *watches, worriedly.*]

P.R. MAN [*O.O.V.*]: O.K., gentlemen – here we go. [*Pause.*] As you'll see from your press releases, last *Friday* Keith Nicholson was a £7-a-week coal-miner. Last *Saturday*, he correctly forecast eight draws on Littlewoods Treble Chance Pool. *Today*, the 27th of September, 1961, he's here, with his charming wife, Vivian, to receive the cheque that has changed their lives . . .

    [KEITH *and* VIVIAN *stare at each other, swallowing their fear.*]

To present it, on behalf of Littlewoods Pools, I've great pleasure in introducing to you – the star of the London Palladium – Mr Bruce Forsyth!

    [*From the reception room we hear applause, muffled voices, noise and bustle.*]

KEITH: Never heard of him.

VIVIAN: Faffs about on the telly. A comic. You've seen him.

P.R. GIRL: Ready, Mr Nicholson?

    [*They both ignore her.*]

VIVIAN [*to* KEITH]: *I* look rough? Cheeky bastard – even your bloody face is shaking. [*She retches slightly.*] That's the scampi coming back . . . [*She takes another swig from a nearby bottle.*]

P.R. GIRL: O.K. Mr Nicholson, Mrs Nicholson. This is it.

VIVIAN: Can't they just give it us in here?

P.R. GIRL: A few nice photographs, that's all. You'll enjoy it.

P.R. MAN [*O.O.V.*]: And now, to receive his cheque for one hundred and fifty two thousand, three hundred and nineteen pounds – the happy winner, Mr Keith Nicholson, and his even happier wife, Vivian!

P.R. GIRL: O.K.?
> [*She helps them to their feet.*
> KEITH *and* VIVIAN *stumble their way to the door – anything but happy.*]

2. Int. Reception room, Dorchester Hotel.
(Continuous in time.)

[*From the photographers' P.O.V., we see* KEITH *and* VIVIAN *enter. Their faces are illuminated by a barrage of flashbulbs. They're blinded, confused and even more frightened.*
Hold tight on their faces throughout the scene.]

FIRST REPORTER [*O.O.V.*]: What are you going to do with the money, Keith?
> [KEITH *opens his mouth to speak – but can't.*]

SECOND REPORTER [*O.O.V.*]: What about *you*, Vivian?

VIVIAN [*barely audible*]: I don't know.

FIRST REPORTER [*O.O.V.*]: Say anything. Whatever comes in your head . . .

VIVIAN: I haven't thought . . . I don't . . .

SECOND REPORTER [*O.O.V.*]: A hundred and fifty two thousand quid, love! What do you *think* you'll do?
> [VIVIAN *stands, helpless.*]

FIRST REPORTER [*O.O.V.*]: Come on, Vivian!
> [VIVIAN – *abruptly, wildly, almost hysterically – yells what she thinks is what they want to hear.*]

VIVIAN: I'm going to spend, spend, spend!!!
> [*Freeze tight on her face – distorted as she yells the words. Over this superimpose titles.*]

3. Ext. Back alley behind Wallington Street, Castleford.
Evening (1950).

[*An extremely poor, working-class street of terraced houses.*
Along the street exhaustedly pushing a rusty, decrepit bike towards
her parents' house, is VIVIAN *at the age of fourteen. The bike is*
laden with sacks of coal-slack. VIVIAN *is filthy and dressed in ill-*
fitting, worn clothes.]

VIVIAN [*V.O.*]: I was born in 1936, in Castleford, Yorkshire. You'll find it on the map. *I'm* the bugger that put
it there. [*Pause.*] Where we lived, all the fellers were coal-
miners. Except my dad. *He* was a full-time, fully-paid-up
bastard. [*She stops at one of the houses and parks the bike outside*
before going in.]

4. Int. Back room, Wallington Street.
(Continuous in time.)

[VIVIAN'S DAD – *all six feet two inches of him – is standing at*
the mantelpiece, using it as a table. He's eating bread and dripping
and drinking from a pint mug of tea.
The other children (all younger than VIVIAN) *are scattered about*
the room, eating, fighting or yelling. These are JESS *and* MAUREEN,
GEORGE *and* GEOFF.
VIVIAN'S MOTHER – *harrassed, long-suffering – is trying to*
maintain some order, tidiness and peace, while making sure the kids
are eating properly.
The room is poverty-stricken but clean.]

VIVIAN [*V.O.*]: My dad always fed his face off the mantelpiece. He said it was because he never knew where the
chairs were because my Mam changed them round so
much. *I* think she did it to make the bugs dizzy . . .
    [VIVIAN *wheels the bike in.*
    DAD *swivels round on hearing her.*]

DAD: Aye, aye, it's landed! Speedy bloody Gonzales.

VIVIAN: What's up with *you*?

DAD: How long's it take to swipe a bit of coal, you lazy cow!

VIVIAN: Can I have summat to eat, Mam?

MOTHER: When you've washed your hands, cock.

VIVIAN: I'm clemming! I've been scraping slack off the tip!

MOTHER: That's what I'm saying . . .

> [MOTHER *turns her back to attend to one of the other kids.*
> VIVIAN *takes the opportunity to pinch a piece of bread from
> one of the smaller kids. The kid promptly starts crying.*
> VIVIAN *belts him across the head.*]

DAD: Well, our Vivian!!?

VIVIAN: Well, what?

DAD [*holding out his palm for money*]: Don't act so bloody
gormless! My beer money!

VIVIAN: I've only just loaded up! I haven't had time to
flog it yet.

DAD: Out! Go on! [*He strides to the door, and opens it for her.*]
Get it sold, you lazy cow!

MOTHER: Don't shout at her, love . . .

DAD [*reasonably*]: Quite right, love. My mistake. I won't.
[*He promptly clouts* VIVIAN *viciously across the head – then
bellows at her.*] Your dad's beer money!!

5. Ext. Back alley behind Wallington Street, Castleford.
A few minutes later.

[VIVIAN *is tearfully wheeling the bike back down the street.*]

VIVIAN [*V.O.*]: I wish we'd have won the pools in *them* days.
I'd have bought him a bloody punch-bag and had a day
off . . .

6 Int. Mother's bedroom, Wallington Street.
Same night.

[There are two beds in the room. In one of them is VIVIAN'S MOTHER, *coughing asthmatically. In the other are* VIVIAN, JESS *and* MAUREEN. JESS *and* MAUREEN *are fast asleep.* VIVIAN *is wide awake and staring up at the ceiling.]*

VIVIAN [*V.O.*]: He was right, mind you – I *was* a lazy cow. I was never up before six. And all I had to do was boil the washing, get the kids up, wash them, dress them, climb up a ladder to wash the windows, blacklead the fire-grate, run errands, work in the pea-fields, pinch coal and go to school. A right lazy cow: the only thing I *didn't* do was give bloody *milk*!

7. Int. Back room, Wallington Street.
(Continuous in time.)

*[*DAD *is turning out the lights, ready to go to bed.]*
VIVIAN [*V.O.*]: My dad was too busy to work. Half the time he was on Lloyd George, and the other half in clink.

8. Int. Mother's bedroom, Wallington Street.
(Continuous in time.)

*[*MOTHER, VIVIAN, MAUREEN *and* JESS *in bed.]*

VIVIAN [*V.O.*]: *He* had epilepsy, and my mam had asthma. [*Pause.*] If they both had a spasm at the same time, it sounded like the kids' matinée at *Gunfight at the O.K. Corral.*
  *[*VIVIAN *looks up.*
  DAD *pops his head in at the door.]*

DAD: I'll say goodnight, then.

MOTHER [*lying in bed*]: Goodnight, love.

>*[He exits again.* MOTHER *lies still till she hears him banging about in the other bedroom. Sure now that he's safely out of the way, she stealthily creeps out of bed, and drags packets of tea and sugar from underneath it. She then opens up a corner of the mattress and starts stuffing the packets inside.*
>
>*Cut to* VIVIAN, *watching her, deadpan.*]

VIVIAN [*V.O.*]: She used to hide *everything*, did my Mam. So's he wouldn't pinch it for beer and Woodbines. We were a great family for trying to hide stuff. Mind you, we'd have got no medals for *succeeding* . . .

9. Int. Back room, Wallington Street.
The next day (1950).

>[DAD *is knocking the contents of the kitchen shelves all over the floor in angry frustration.*
>
>VIVIAN *stands watching – almost in tears.*]

DAD: All right, mard-arse! Where's she hidden them?

VIVIAN [*fearfully*]: I don't know.

>[DAD *clouts her across the head.*]

DAD: I'm your bloody father! You're supposed to *love* me!

>[*He clouts her again.*]

VIVIAN: I bet she definitely hasn't sewn them in the mattress . . .

10. Int. Mother's bedroom, Wallington Street.
A few minutes later.

>[DAD *is sitting on the floor, ripping the mattress open. He pulls out the packets of tea and sugar.*
>
>VIVIAN *is beside him, emptying the tea into one big bag, and the sugar into another.*]

Meanwhile, DAD *fills the empty packets with coal-slack from a coal scuttle. He stuffs the coal-filled tea and sugar packets back into the mattress.*
Over this:]

VIVIAN [*V.O.*]: 'Love' him? I hated his guts! His arguing, his boozing, his thumping. He was an ignorant bastard. I bloody hated him. [*Pause.*] Which is why I *did* love him, I suppose. Can't have one without the other, can you? If you hate someone when they're being a bastard to you, it proves you love them, doesn't it? Otherwise you wouldn't give a monkey's *how* big a bastard they was.

DAD: Right. Sew it up again. [*He hands her the bags of tea and sugar.*] Get them flogged. Bring me the brass. And keep your trap shut to your mam. She has enough aggravation.

VIVIAN [*with exaggerated, childlike sarcasm*]: Go on! *Does* she? Who from?

[DAD *promptly clouts her again for her impudence.*]

11. Int. Luxury bedroom. The Grosvenor Hotel, London.
Night (1961).

[*The blow delivered at the end of the previous scene lands on the face of* KEITH *as he enters the room. He's still dressed in his brand-new clothes, and he's merrily tipsy.*
VIVIAN, *who's just delivered the smack, is stonily sober and furious. She's wearing a black bra and black panties.*]

KEITH: What the hell's that for???

VIVIAN: If that's what money does for you, I'll burn the bugger!

KEITH: What money? I've only had it half a sodding day!

VIVIAN: Showing me up...

KEITH: What doing?

VIVIAN: *You* know.

KEITH: I don't!

VIVIAN: Well, *I* do!

[*She furiously continues doing what she was doing before he came in – polishing the mirrors.*

KEITH *watches her, puzzled.*]

KEITH: What are *you* doing?

[*She ignores him.*]

They have chambermaids for that . . .

VIVIAN: I saw you, Keith Nicholson! Pegging up chorus-girls' legs . . . eyes stuck out like chapel hat-pegs.

KEITH: When?

VIVIAN: 'When?', he says! Tonight! With half the sodding Palladium watching you!

KEITH: I couldn't help myself, you daft bat! *We're* on the front row, and *they're* kicking them in the air! What were I supposed to to – shut my eyes?

VIVIAN: You didn't gawp at Sammy Davis like that . . .

[KEITH *laughs. Sits on the edge of the bed, taking his shoes off.*]

KEITH: *All* the fellers were looking, love . . . all the Little-woods lot . . . I did nowt wrong . . .

VIVIAN: I'd have gouged your eyes *out*, if you had!

[*She continues polishing the mirrors.*

KEITH *starts undressing, still watching her, puzzled.*]

KEITH: I wish I knew what the hell you were doing!

VIVIAN: What's it look like?

KEITH: What's it *for*?

[*She turns to face him, smiles sexily and comes towards him. She puts her arms round his waist.*]

VIVIAN [*quietly, sexily*]: We're rich now, lover-boy. We can do anything we want. We can lie in bed and rub pound notes all over each other. A hundred and fifty thousand of them . . .

KEITH [*laughs*]: We'd have a job! It's in a cheque.

VIVIAN: We'll cash it.

KEITH: The bank's got it.

VIVIAN: We'll draw it out.

KEITH: They're shut.

> [*The above five speeches are said smilingly, teasingly – a sort of gentle sexual foreplay.*]

VIVIAN: Fair do's. We'll pour Dubonnet over each other instead. [*Smiles.*] Then lick it off.

KEITH [*half amused, half excited*]: Is that right?

> [*She nods towards the bedside table. It's covered with bottles of liqueurs.*]

VIVIAN: I've got them in ready.

KEITH [*looking*]: Crikey! How much did that lot come to?

VIVIAN [*grins*]: Who cares?

> [*They move into a close embrace.*]

KEITH: I still don't know what the mirrors are for . . .

VIVIAN: All the better to see you with.

KEITH: What doing?

VIVIAN: With our money, we can afford a good view . . .

> [*She promptly starts tearing his clothes off, laughing, then grabs bottles and starts pouring their contents over his bared chest.*
>
> *Pan away from them, round the room, which is littered with a mass of expensively wrapped purchases.*
>
> *Over this*:]

VIVIAN [*O.O.V.*]: We'll have the best sexual happening of all time . . .

KEITH [*O.O.V.*]: The best what??

VIVIAN [*O.O.V.*]: You heard.

KEITH [*O.O.V.*]: That's not what *I* call it.

VIVIAN: Dirty sod . . .

12. Ext. Playing field, Castleford. Day (1950).

[*The playing field is a third-rate football pitch. Bumpy, unkempt, probably without goalposts.*
A gang of boys are playing a scratch game of football.

Standing watching them, adoringly, longingly, is the fourteen-year-old VIVIAN. *She wears very tatty, patched clothes. Her hair is plaited and parted in the middle. Her face is very pimpled. Her lips are badly and thicky daubed with lipstick.*

A couple of GIRLFRIENDS *are with her. They're rather more smartly dressed and their hair isn't in pigtails. But they're similarly daubed with lipstick.*]

VIVIAN [*V.O.*]: I was a right ugly pig as a child. In them days, the greatest thing in life was getting a lad to whistle at you. I was dead useless at it. I got sod-all. The other lasses did, but they had proper clothes – and they didn't have plaits. [*Pause.*] My dad wouldn't let me cut mine off. They were sacred to him, them plaits. [*Pause.*] They were a bloody menace to me. So was my chest. So were my pimples. Everything about me.

[*The three girls are trying, without success, to attract some attention from the boys.*

The ball rolls to the touchline. VIVIAN *picks it up excitedly, while one of the boys runs over to collect it from her. She smiles what she fondly hopes is a seductive smile at him. The boy completely ignores the smile, takes the ball from her, winks at one of the other girls and gives a low wolf-whistle.*]

GIRL [*delighted*]: Cheeky bugger . . .

[*The boy takes a throw-in to restart the game. The game continues.*]

GIRL [*satisfied, to* VIVIAN]: I've got to get home now.

[*The news is a terrible blow to* VIVIAN. *Her heart sinks even further.*]

VIVIAN: Not yet!

GIRL: I've stuff to do.

[*They start to walk away, with* VIVIAN *hopelessly glancing back from time to time at the boys.*

When they're some distance away, VIVIAN *and the* GIRL *take sheets of paper from their pockets. With the paper, they rub leg make-up from their legs and the lipstick from their mouths. As* VIVIAN *pulls more paper from her pocket, a small cheap manicure box is dragged out with it, and falls to the ground. The* GIRL *sees it.*]

GIRL: What's that?

[VIVIAN *hastily grabs the box and shoves it back in her pocket.*]

VIVIAN: Nowt.

GIRL: Yes, it is.

VIVIAN: No, it isn't!

[*The* GIRL *tries to pull it out of her pocket.* VIVIAN *fights her off.*]

GIRL: Have you nicked it?

VIVIAN [*passionately, almost tearfully*]: She promised it me! She's promised it me for months! Every time I scrub her stinking house out, every week, she promises!

GIRL: Who?

VIVIAN: My stinking grandma.

GIRL: So have you nicked it?

VIVIAN: I've cleaned all sorts to get that ... the petty, everything. A promise is a promise.

[*She takes the box from her pocket and shows it to the* GIRL. *The* GIRL *opens it. We see that it's a cheap manicure set.*]

VIVIAN: It's for doing fingernails.

GIRL: It's bonny isn't it?

VIVIAN [*gravely*]: It's the beautifullest thing I've ever seen. [*A pause.*]

GIRL: What if she sees you with it?

VIVIAN: She won't. I'm going to hide the bastard.

13. Int. Back room, Wallington Street. Same night.

[VIVIAN's MOTHER, *coughing bronchitically, is changing the furniture round.*
VIVIAN *is doing the family ironing.*
O.O.V., *we hear* DAD *enter the house, singing tipsily.*
VIVIAN *and her* MOTHER *exchange sardonic glances.*

DAD *bursts in, full of somewhat embarrassing, drunken, sentimental bonhomie.*]

DAD: There they are! The lights of my life!

MOTHER [*drily, resignedly*]: Rent money boozed again, then, is it?

DAD: I love you two, you know that, don't you? I don't love many buggers, but I love you two!

MOTHER: Aye ... peeing a week's rent money down the Miners Arms pee-stone ...

DAD [*amused*]: Give us a kiss then!

[MOTHER *wearily offers her cheek to be kissed. He kisses her, then happily lumbers over to* VIVIAN. *He kisses her. She winces at his smelly breath.*]

VIVIAN: What's your scent called, then ... Bouquet of Tetley's Brewery?

DAD: You what, cock?

MOTHER: Your breath smells.

DAD [*martyredly, to* VIVIAN]: That's not the beer, love. It's worry. Worry causes bad breath. It's a well known medical fact. [*He switches immediately and without warning, to his vicious, aggressive alter ego.*] What the hell have you got on?!!

[*He's glaring at her short skirt. She follows his eyes.*]

VIVIAN [*defensively*]: How d'you mean?

DAD: Pull the bastard down!

MOTHER: Leave her alone, love.

DAD: Showing all you've got!

VIVIAN: They *wear* them this length ...!

[*He clouts her across the head.*]

MOTHER: For God's sake!

DAD: She's got bloody lipstick on!!! [*In his eyes, it's the cardinal sin; nothing could disgust or enrage him more.*]

VIVIAN [*rubbing her lips guiltily*]: I haven't, Mum!

DAD: You pigging have!

VIVIAN: My lips are chapped ... They got chapped watching the lads ...

DAD [*even more horrified*]: *What* lads??

VIVIAN: Playing footer...

DAD: I see. [*pause.*] Skirt halfway up your arse, cracking on it's a scarf. Lipstick. Lads. [*Pause.*] You're going the right way, aren't you?

MOTHER: Here we go...

DAD: [*to* VIVIAN]: For the hundredth bloody time – what happens if you stand kissing lads down back alleys!

VIVIAN: Who've I kissed??

DAD [*screaming*]: It makes you bloody pregnant!

VIVIAN: I haven't kissed no one!

DAD: Pregnant!!

VIVIAN: Just kissing?

DAD: And when you're pregnant, you're finished! Your life's finished!

VIVIAN [*to* MOTHER]: It isn't kissing that does it, is it, Mam?

MOTHER: *I* don't know!

VIVIAN: It's time you found out then! There's a bloody houseful of us!

DAD [*to* VIVIAN]: Bed!

[VIVIAN *starts to leave the room to go to bed.*]

Come here!

[*She goes to him. He smashes her across the head.*]

14. Int. Mother's bedroom, Wallington Street.
Night (1950).

[VIVIAN *is in bed with* JESS *and* MAUREEN. VIVIAN *is awake, the others asleep.*

VIVIAN *has a slice of bread and jam. She's biting pieces out of it, to shape it into the profile of a face. She then holds the bread to the half light to make the shadow of a boy's face on the wall.*]

VIVIAN [*V.O.*]: No one can belt you for thinking, though. Imagining. [*Pause.*] Like – who would I marry, for instance. And would he be bonny, and would he have a trade in his fingers, and would he treat me right . . .?

[*She kisses the mouth of the bread-face, then eats up all the bread.*]

I was safe in bed. At least, I *thought* I was. That night, though, while I was in sodding dreamland, my dad lit a fire in the grate A dirty big fire roaring up the chimney . . .

15. Int. Back room, Wallington Street.
The next morning.

[*Open on the grate piled high with dead ashes.*
Still wearing a ragged nightie, straight from bed, VIVIAN *bursts into the room – and, horrified, sees the ashes. She races to the grate, and almost in tears, she pushes her hand up the chimney. She brings down the remains of her manicure-box . . . blackened, burnt and ruined.*]

VIVIAN [*V.O.*]: It was only where I'd hidden my box for doing fingernails, wasn't it? I told you we were the world's worst at hiding stuff . . .

[VIVIAN *opens the box and looks, heartbroken, at the charred melted mess.*]

It was all I'd ever wanted in my life, that box. It was the beautifullest thing I'd ever seen. It still *is*, in a way. [*Pause.*] It must've cost all of one and six in Woolworths.

16. Ext. Working-class streets, Castleford.
Day (1961).

[*A taxi is driving along through the streets. Inside are the* DRIVER, KEITH, VIVIAN *and the expensively-wrapped parcels we saw in Scene 11.*]

17. Int. Travelling taxi. (Continuous in time.)

[*The* DRIVER *talks to them over his shoulder – as though he's sure they're wrong, but far be it from him to contradict.*]

DRIVER: You're sure it's Kershaw Avenue you want?

KEITH: Hundred and thirteen.

DRIVER: Never much call for us lads down Kershaw Avenue...

VIVIAN [*enjoying his puzzlement*]: No?

DRIVER: It's virgin territory as a rule.

KEITH [*to* VIVIAN]: It's what?

VIVIAN [*irritated*]: Not what *you* mean...

DRIVER: Different again today, by all accounts. Crawling with newspaper fellers...

VIVIAN [*suddenly concerned*]: Is it?

DRIVER: So I've heard. Some jammy pig's won a million pounds or summat...

KEITH [*amused*]: Go on?

DRIVER: So I've heard. A million... two million. Summat like that.

KEITH: Not *three* million?

DRIVER: Everyone's got a different tale. I'm not a betting man myself.

KEITH [*enjoying himself*]: Me neither.
   [*A pause*].

DRIVER: I expect his missus'll do it in for him. She's a right little tart by all accounts.

KEITH: Oh, aye?

DRIVER: So I've heard.

VIVIAN: Me too.

KEITH [*niggled*]: Well, *I've* heard different.

VIVIAN [*suddenly*]: Hang on!
   [*The* DRIVER *brakes hard.*]

DRIVER: What've I hit?
   [*We see* REPORTERS *down street.*]

VIVIAN: Can you cut down Langton Street and up the *other* end of Kershaw Avenue? Number eight.

DRIVER: Not a hundred and thirteen?

KEITH [*to* VIVIAN]: Your mam's??

VIVIAN: I had enough of reporters at the airport. Life's too short.

[*Immediate cut to:*]

18. Int. Parents' back room, Kershaw Avenue.
Night (1961).

[*The sideboard is covered with bottles – liqueurs, spirits and beer. The room is littered with the debris of a party.*
Sitting or lying around are VIVIAN, MOTHER, DAD, VIVIAN'S *brothers and sisters and one or two neighbours. Those who aren't drunkenly asleep are drunkenly (but tiredly) singing.*
There's a loud knocking at the front door.]

VIVIAN: For crying out loud . . . three o'clock in the sodding morning! Don't they ever give up?

MOTHER: It's been all day the same. If it's not newspapers, it's the neighbours. Everybody. I've been half expecting bloody coach trips! And my head with the noise . . .! God bless Cephos Powders . . .
    [*More loud knocking.*]

DAD: If it's the bobbies again, slip them a couple of bottles . .
    [MOTHER *gets up and peers tentatively through the curtains.*]

MOTHER: Your Keith.

DAD [*tipsily, happily expansive*]: Let him in, then, lass! Let the lad in!
    [VIVIAN *glances at* DAD, *wryly.*]

VIVIAN: Bloody hell . . .

DAD: What?

VIVIAN: You'd give him house-room now, would you?

DAD: Who?

VIVIAN: Good enough to darken your door-step all of a sudden . . .

DAD: What are you on about?

VIVIAN: I'm just trying to fathom what might have changed your attitude, that's all . . . [*a beat*] . . . you smarmy old sod!

DAD [*evasively*]: *I'll* let him in. Good lad is our Keith . . .
[*He exits.*

> MOTHER *has meanwhile returned to the table to sit with* VIVIAN. *As they say the following dialogue,* MOTHER *fondly strokes a length of curtain material, still half-wrapped in its wrapping-paper.* VIVIAN *smilingly watches her. A tender, close moment between them. Perhaps the first there's ever been: possibly the last.*]

VIVIAN [*gently*]: All right, then, Flower?

> [MOTHER *smiles back at her . . . near to tears.*]

MOTHER: Who'd have thought it, eh, Viv?

VIVIAN: Been a fair night, hasn't it?

MOTHER: All day I haven't known whether to laugh or to cry . . . When I think back . . . And then when I saw your photo in the paper . . . In London and everything . . . I still can't believe it . . .

VIVIAN: Oh, mam . . .

> [*They start to laugh and cry, quietly, happily, arms round each other.*
>
> DAD *and* KEITH *enter:* DAD *with an unaccustomed arm round* KEITH'S *shoulder.*]

DAD: Here he is! The man himself! [*To* MOTHER] Get up, let him sit down.

> [MOTHER *automatically gets up:* KEITH *automatically takes her chair.*]

VIVIAN [*to* KEITH]: Have they gone?

KEITH: There were two left from the *News of the World*. I gave them a drink and a quote, and they buggered off.

DAD: A drink and a what?

VIVIAN [*getting up*]: We'll make tracks, then. Did you give the kids their pressies?

KEITH: They were asleep. I thought we'd wait while morning.

[*He gets up, ready to go, as* VIVIAN *gathers up her coat, handbag etc.*
DAD *is watching her, concerned.*]
DAD: Viv . . . Keith . . . I wanted a word with you . . .
VIVIAN: We've *been* here long enough!
DAD: No . . . private. Come in the kitchen.
[*He exits into kitchen.*
VIVIAN *and* KEITH *exchange a brief, knowing glance.*]

19. Int. Parents' kitchen, Kershaw Avenue.
(Continuous in time.)

[DAD *has entered from the living room.*
VIVIAN *follows him in, carrying her parcels and struggling into her coat.*
KEITH *follows.*
MOTHER *enters during the opening dialogue, and puts the kettle on.*]

VIVIAN [*to* DAD]: If you're going to make a speech, I'd best go and change my knickers . . .
DAD [*pained*]: Now was that called for? There's no need for bloody language, sweetheart . . .
VIVIAN [*wryly, to* KEITH]: 'Sweetheart'. [*To* DAD] Go on then.
[VIVIAN *and* KEITH *face him and stand waiting.*]
DAD [*uncomfortably*]: Well, nothing, really . . . no, I were just studying to myself, like, about financial arrangements and that . . .
VIVIAN: What financial arrangements?
[DAD *squirms a little more.*]
DAD: Well . . . re finance, really . . . Like, well, the money, sort of style. What you're contemplating arranging, sort of thing . . . [*Needled*] You know what I mean!
KEITH: I've to see Martin's Bank in the morning. They're sorting it out. Money for the kids and so forth . . .

VIVIAN: And five hundred for you, Mam.

MOTHER: Five hundred what?

VIVIAN: Five hundred pounds.

MOTHER: Oh, no, love – I couldn't! I've got the curtaining material you brought me! I don't want money, Viv!

KEITH: Well, you're having it.

MOTHER: I draw National Assistance – I'm not allowed money in the bank . . .

DAD: Well, sew it in the mattress, you gormless sod! [*to* VIVIAN] She'll have it, she'll have it. [*To* MOTHER] It's nothing to them! They'll have plenty left out of hundred and fifty thousand. [*Smiles ingratiatingly at* VIVIAN.] Won't you, cock?

> [VIVIAN *isn't fooled for a second. This is a moment she's been looking forward to almost since they got the cheque, the day before.*]

VIVIAN: Don't bother sucking up, Dad. We've already decided what *you're* getting.

DAD [*beaming, relieved*]: Good lass.

KEITH: Sod all.

> [DAD *stares at her, then at* KEITH, *incredulously. They beam back at him. A pause.*]

DAD: You what?

VIVIAN: I'll spell it for you. S.O.D. A – double –

DAD: You're giving me *nothing*? ? ?

KEITH: With knobs on.

VIVIAN: Happy?

DAD: I'm your bloody father! !

VIVIAN: I remember.

DAD: I brought you up!

VIVIAN: I'll say you did.

MOTHER [*sighing*]: Oh, hell . . . I shall need that five hundred pound. He'll start smashing the house up . . .

> [*A pause.* DAD *struggles with his emotions.*]

DAD [*gravely, humbly*]: You've been very honest with me, Vivian. I respect that.

VIVIAN: Thank you.

DAD: Thank *you*.
　　[*He immediately wheels round and starts smashing up every-thing on the kitchen shelves.*
　　VIVIAN *and* KEITH *at once start to exit through the back door.*]
VIVIAN [*shouts above the noise of the demolition*]: You'll get your beer and Woodbines, you bloody deadleg! I won't see you short!
　　[KEITH *and* VIVIAN *exit.*]

30. Int. Hall. Vivian's house, Kershaw Avenue.
A few minutes later. Night.

[*The hall is in darkness.*
We hear VIVIAN *and* KEITH *approaching outside. The door opens:* KEITH *and* VIVIAN *enter with their parcels.*
The floor is littered with scores of envelopes.]

VIVIAN: Bloody hell! Castleford Post Office . . .
KEITH: There's another dustbin-full in the yard. I'll clear this lot in the morning.
　　[VIVIAN *stands gazing down at the envelopes.*]
VIVIAN: Marvellous, isn't it? When have *we* ever had a letter – bar reminders and final demands?
KEITH: The Littlewoods chap says we've to burn them.

21. Int. Bedroom. Vivian's house, Kershaw Avenue.
Twenty minutes or so later.

[KEITH *and* VIVIAN *are in bed.*
KEITH *is almost completely exhausted and struggling to get to sleep.*
VIVIAN *is selecting and reading letters which she takes at random from an enormous pile scattered over the bed.*]

FIRST WOMAN'S VOICE [*as* VIVIAN *reads*]: Dear Mr and

Mrs Nicholson, I hope you don't mind me writing, as my only son, Clifford, was a lance-corporal in the East Lancashires in the war. He died for his King and Country on the 8th of November, 1944, in Germany where he is now buried. I have been saving up ever since to go to see his grave, only I still need another twelve pounds nearly. I would be eternally grateful if you could see your way to helping me. I have never asked for money in my life, and have always kept a clean home. God bless you. Please excuse pencil.

[VIVIAN *puts the letter down, opens another envelope and starts reading.*]

FIRST MAN'S VOICE: Dear Mrs Nicholson, I have a haulage business near St Albans. Unfortunately, through lack of capital, it has unfortunately gone bankrupt. However, should you wish to become a co-director, then with your capital and my –

[VIVIAN *throws it down and picks up a leaflet.*]

VIVIAN [*reading*]: 'Switch to Gas!' [*She puts it down and picks up another leaflet.*] [*Reading*] 'Remember you're a miner – don't change from coal to gas!' [*She puts it down and picks up a letter.*]

SECOND MAN'S VOICE: 'Thy money perish with thee', Apostles, chapter 8, verse 20. I hope you stink and rot in hell, you lousy bastards!

[VIVIAN *puts it down, hastily, and picks up another.*]

SECOND WOMAN'S VOICE: Dear Mrs Nicholson, I don't want money. I'm writing to you, because as a mother of four children, you'll understand. I have five. My husband is in Wakefield prison for not paying the HP on our washer – which was a Vactric Tumble-Action Automatic. Please can you send me your childrens' old clothes . . .

VIVIAN: They've got none, chuck. All they've got is what they're wearing, with their arses hanging out . . .

KEITH [*almost asleep*]: Uh?

[VIVIAN *picks up another letter.*]

THIRD WOMAN'S VOICE: Dear Pools Lady, I am 82 years

of age. I can remember Queen Victoria. In recent years I have never been lonely, because of my cat. My lovely cat was my constant companion. He was called Donald, after Donald Peers the singer. He died the Wednesday after Whit Monday, aged thirteen and a half. Can you please buy me a pot one, an ornament of a cat, so I can sit it on the hearth and talk to it?

[VIVIAN *slowly puts the letter down.*]

VIVIAN: Keith?

KEITH: Uh?

VIVIAN: How much is a pot cat?

KEITH [*drenched in sleep*]: I'm burning the buggers in the morning. Get to sleep!

[VIVIAN *shovels all the letters onto the floor, turns the light out and snuggles down in bed. A pause.*]

VIVIAN [*quietly*]: I feel nervous.

KEITH: What about?

VIVIAN: I don't know. [*She puts her arms round him.*] Keith?

KEITH: I can't, love.

VIVIAN: 'Night, then.

[*The only reply* KEITH *can manage is a sleepy grunt. A pause.*]

I'm going to have champagne and bacon butties for breakfast. If we've any bacon.

22. Int. Matthew's bedroom. Night (1952).

[*In the bed,* VIVIAN *is in the arms of a naked man. She's also naked.*]

VIVIAN [*V.O.*]: My dad was wrong about what happens if you kiss a lad. I found a more sure way of getting pregnant, sure-fire, guaranteed. *Nicer*, an' all . . . [*Pause.*] I know it sounds romantic and daft . . . but the loveliest thing about it was just feeling someone's *skin* next to you. Just bare skin touching *your* bare skin. I think it's the loveliest feeling there is. And it's free. Even if you have nowt, you can be happy. Skin against skin. Nothing's ever made me as happy. It was my first sexual happening.

[*They turn over in bed. For the first time we see the man's face: it's* MATTHEW.]

His name was Matthew. He was twenty-three and barmy. Barmy for wanting to marry me. I were sweet sixteen, a cinema-usherette, and barmier still for accepting.

23. Int. 'The Kiosk' dance hall. Evening (1952).

[*A cheap, tatty dance-hall.*
Among the couples smooching to a foxtrot are VIVIAN *and* MATTHEW.
She glances at other men while she's dancing with him. She's now more smartly-dressed. Her hair is in a bubble-cut.]

VIVIAN [*V.O.*]: I didn't love Matthew. I didn't even *like* him. The second time we went to bed, I didn't even like his *skin*. [*Pause.*] All the lads fancied me by then ... because of my bubble-cut. *I* fancied *them* an' all. Bubble-cuts were miles behind the times before my dad let me have one. I didn't care if it was a hundred years behind the times ... I loved that bubble-cut. [*A pause.*] Anyroad, we met in the January and were wed in April. Married in the morning, and regretting it by dinner-time. By the time the chip shops were shut, I was fancying anything in trousers. Anything bar him.

24. Int. Front and back room, Matthew's house. Evening (1954).

[MATTHEW, *after a day's work down the pit, is at the back room table, eating.*
VIVIAN *is in a chair, angrily smoking a cigarette.*

From time to time, they exchange cold, hostile looks.
VIVIAN *gets up and calmly exits.*
MATTHEW *ignores her and continues eating.*]

VIVIAN [*V.O.*]: There was nothing between us. It weren't a marriage at all, really. It was nothing. No *fire* in it.
   [VIVIAN *goes to front room with a can of paraffin. She calmly pours it over the settee.*]
So, one night, I got some organized . . .
   [*She takes a box of matches, strikes one and drops it onto the settee. The settee bursts into flames.*
   MATTHEW *comes into front room.*]
MATTHEW: Christ Almighty ! ! !
VIVIAN [*calmly*]: Turned out warmer, hasn't it?
MATTHEW: Put it out ! !
VIVIAN: Don't be like that. I've only just lit the bugger.
   [MATTHEW *races out to the back.*
   VIVIAN *stands watching the settee fiercely burning.*]
[*V.O.*] I was married in white – three months gone with our Stephen. We had a page-boy, six bridesmaids and eleven gallons of beer in a barrel. [*Pause.*] I didn't shut my eyes once the night before the wedding . . . worrying was I doing the right thing. My dad couldn't sleep neither. Knowing there was eleven gallons of Tetley's arriving in the morning, he spent all night bloody whistling. [*Pause*]. I cried in church. I even prayed. When they say that bit about does anyone know any just impediment, I were praying everybody would shout '*I* do!'
   [MATTHEW *re-enters with a bucket of water. He throws the water ineffectually over the fire.*]
[*Angrily*] What the hell do you think you're doing ! !
MATTHEW: The bloody suite, woman!
VIVIAN: It's *mine*! I paid for it! Leave it!
   [*He obeys, and stands, helplessly, watching it burn.*
   VIVIAN'*s eyes fill with tears.*]
[*V.O.*] I'd worked hard for that three-piece suite. Worked and saved. It were a lovely piece of furniture.

And he let me burn it. See what I mean? Why didn't he kick hell out of me? He just wouldn't. Even when I told him I had necking sessions every night on my way home with lads from work. [*Pause.*] He was happy just loving me, was Matthew. Letting me do what I wanted. What made *him* happy was seeing *me* happy. Well, that's not love, is it? That's not man and wife. That's no marriage, isn't that . . .

25. Ext. Backyard, Matthew's house. The next morning.

[*In the yard is an old pram. Inside the pram is baby Stephen.*
The charred frame of the settee comes hurtling out of the kitchen doorway.
VIVIAN *follows behind, sweeping out the burnt ashes of the upholstery.*]

VIVIAN [*V.O.*]: My marriage was dead. Ashes to bloody ashes.
  [*The baby starts crying. She goes over to him and rocks the pram. Irritatedly.*]
VIVIAN: Shut your bloody cake-hole!
  [*V.O.*] Seventeen years old, with a kid. I was only a kid myself! You enjoy yourself once . . . and that's what you get for it: bloody baby-minding for the rest of my life. Learning to be an old woman. [*Pause.*] I once thought I'd give anything to see the world, so I wrote up to join the NAAFI. But I think you'd to be eighteen.
  [*Cut, from* VIVIAN's *P.O.V., to see* KEITH *– aged seventeen – climbing along their dividing yard wall, holding a pigeon.*
  VIVIAN's *heart leaps on seeing him. He, too, is very attracted to her.*]
KEITH [*brusquely*]: What are you gawping at?
VIVIAN [*equally brusquely*]: Not much.
KEITH [*more brusquely*]: Do you want a photograph or summat?

174

VIVIAN [*more brusquely still*]: You'd bust the camera.

[*V.O.*] I thought my life was over. It were only just starting.

[KEITH *continues attending to his pigeon.*

VIVIAN *continues attending to the debris of the settee, glancing very briefly and surreptitiously at him a couple of times.*]

His name was Keith and he lived next door with his grandma. [*Pause.*] The minute I saw him, I *knew* it were just starting . . .

26. Ext. Willowbridge Motors, Castleford. Day (1961).

[*Open on a brand-new, gleaming, silver-grey Chevrolet Impala . . . shot spectacularly from a variety of angles, each intercut with shots of* VIVIAN *gazing at it . . . almost like a TV commercial.*

VIVIAN'S *gaze is more than satisfaction or pleasure. This is perhaps the most fulfilling moment of her life. Her gaze is adoring, quietly ecstatic. At this moment she knows with certainty that all that lies ahead is untold happiness. The Chevrolet is her proof.*

(*Note: In this scene her hair is green.*)

KEITH *is standing beside her . . . looking from* VIVIAN *to the car and back again . . . doubtfully.*]

KEITH: And you're sure that's the one you want? [*No reply.*] In your own mind, like? [*No reply.*] It's not too big for you? [*Pause.*] Or anything . . . [*No reply.*] You can't even bloody *drive*!!

VIVIAN: *You* can't.

KEITH: I'm getting a tuppence-ha'penny shooting-brake!

VIVIAN: Tuppence-ha'penny?

KEITH: Well . . .

VIVIAN: We can afford it, man!

KEITH: Two thousand eight hundred quid.

VIVIAN: We can afford a couple of dozen!

KEITH: Plus tax, number plates and delivery charges.
 [*A pause.*]
 I mean, we've to get a new house yet . . .
VIVIAN [*almost reverently*]: I'll never want for anything again
 Keith . . .
KEITH: 'Let's go and look for a new house,' you said.
VIVIAN: First things first, lad.

27. Ext. Castleford Streets or surrounding countryside.
Day (1961).

[*A wide shot. The Chevrolet driving along – at a ferocious speed
and with utter recklessness.*]

VIVIAN [*V.O.*]: It was called a Chevrolet Impala. A chevvy.
 [*Pause.*] I failed four driving tests, and passed on my fifth.
 Keith smashed his shooting-brake up on the way to his
 first test, but passed on his second. I kept my L-plates on
 after I passed, hoping the police'd pick me up – and I
 could spit in their eye. They'd picked me up often enough
 for *not* having them on when I were a learner . . .

28. Int. Travelling Chevrolet. Day.
(Continuous in time.)

[VIVIAN *is driving* . . . *through incongruously poor streets.*
KEITH, *somewhat nervous, is in the passenger seat.*
VIVIAN *is having the time of her life. Suddenly she swerves the car
round a corner.*]
KEITH [*alarmed*]: You're going the wrong way!!
VIVIAN [*happy, calm*]: That's right.
KEITH: Where the hell are you going?
VIVIAN: Ewbank's Sweet Factory.
KEITH: What the hell for??

VIVIAN: I work there, don't I?
KEITH: Not *now* you don't, you soft sod!
VIVIAN [*grinning*]: They still owe me a week's wages ...

29. Int. Keith's Grandma's living room. Evening (1954).

[VIVIAN *and* GRANDMA *are seated at the table, eating stew.
There are half-a-dozen bottles of beer on the table. They're having
a mimed shouting conversation.*]

VIVIAN [*V.O.*]: Well, if Keith lived with his grandma, first
thing on the agenda was to get pally with the grandma,
wasn't it? Feet under the table – bloody sharpish. So I
did. She kept inviting me in for a plate of stew ... horrible, greasy muck it was an' all. Muggins here had to
provide the beer and fags. [*Pause.*] Stone-deaf, she was. A
right old witch. Three evenings on the trot I spent with
her. You know, persevering. Still ... I'd have done it
for three hundred – just to get my hands on her Keith.
My hands on him, my arms round him ... oh, God! ...
and my legs! [*Pause.*] Needless to say, for them three
nights, he wasn't even bloody there ...!

30. Ext. Vivian's new house, Grange Avenue.
Day (1961).

[*The Chevrolet and Vauxhall shooting-brake are parked outside.
The Chevvy is filthy.
Two* WOMEN, *shopping bags in hand, are standing across the
street, gossiping. They look with disgust at the Chevvy and the
house.*]

FIRST WOMAN: Car that size, into the bargain. I don't
think it's ever *seen* soap and water.

SECOND WOMAN: I don't think *she* has. Her kids definitely haven't.

FIRST WOMAN: And they've done nothing with the garden.

SECOND WOMAN: Disgrace.

FIRST WOMAN: Well, they haven't the time really, fair's fair. It's a full-time job is boozing all day.

SECOND WOMAN: I believe they were paralytic in the Miners Arms. Effing and blinding. You'd think they'd ban them . . . but they won't.

FIRST WOMAN: Mrs Danby said the police were round to them three o'clock this morning. Disturbing the peace.

[*A pause. They stand staring at the house with hostility.*]
Beautiful home like that. The furniture chap said it was reeking of vomit . . . Sliding in it.

31. Int. Living room, Vivian's house, Grange Avenue.
(Continuous in time.)

[(*Note: In this scene* VIVIAN's *hair is mauve.*)
In the midst of the debris of a party, VIVIAN *is sitting staring unseeingly out of the window. She feels very lonely and depressed.*
KEITH *enters from the hall, drink in hand. He looks at her, puzzled at her still, sad mood.*]

KEITH: What's up?

VIVIAN: Nothing.

KEITH: What are you looking at?

VIVIAN: Nothing.

KEITH: The Chevvy?

VIVIAN: No, nothing. Just sitting.

KEITH: You've not gone off it, have you?

VIVIAN: Mmm?

KEITH: Have you gone off it?

VIVIAN: Off what?

[*He sighs irritably, impatiently.*]

KEITH: Look, are you bloody coming or not!

VIVIAN: Where?

KEITH: Well, where, you daft bat! They're open!

VIVIAN: I thought I'd tidy up a bit.

KEITH: What for? They'll all be at it again tonight.

[*A pause.*]

VIVIAN: Shall I peel some potatoes?

KEITH: How do you mean?

VIVIAN: For summat to do.

KEITH: You've enough potatoes peeled for a week in there!

[*A pause.*]

VIVIAN: I thought it'd be summat to do.

[*She continues staring morosely out of the window.*

KEITH *exits, annoyed.*

VIVIAN *doesn't even notice.*]

32. Int. Keith's Grandma's living room.
Evening (1954).

[*Same night as scene 29.* VIVIAN *and* GRANDMA *have finished eating stew. They're now smoking cigarettes and drinking beer.*]

VIVIAN [*V.O.*]: Three nights wasted ... Then the fourth night – the Thursday – as she was showing her umpteenth light ale the way to go home – in he came!

[KEITH *enters, he nods curtly at* VIVIAN. *She nods uninterestedly back.*]

God, he was gorgeous ...

GRANDMA: Been playing dominoes?

KEITH [*yelling*]: Darts!

GRANDMA [*can't hear*]: You what?

KEITH [*yelling*]: Darting! [*He mimes throwing darts.*]

GRANDMA [*to* VIVIAN]: It's under age for pubbing it, is sixteen. I've told him. Won't listen. This is our Keith.

VIVIAN [*couldn't care less*]: Oh, aye?

GRANDMA [*to* KEITH]: Do you want summat to eat?

KEITH [*shouting*]: I've had a pie!

GRANDMA [*can't hear*]: I'll make you summat.
> [*She gets up and exits into the kitchen.*
> KEITH *sits down and starts poking his gums with a matchstick.*
> VIVIAN *gazes at him.*]

VIVIAN [*V.O.*]: I hated that habit.

KEITH: What do they call *you*, then?

VIVIAN: Vivian.

KEITH: You've too much lipstick on.
> [VIVIAN *embarrassedly rubs at her lips with her knuckles.*
> KEITH *goes to the mantelpiece for another matchstick for his gums.*
> VIVIAN *goes to him.*]

VIVIAN: It's a nice name is Keith.

KEITH: Vivian isn't. I'll call you summat else. I'll call you Goldie.
> [*Very tentatively, she puts her arms round him. He reciprocates shyly and clumsily.*
> *Cut to* GRANDMA *at the kitchen door. She's seen them. Her eyes narrow.*
> VIVIAN *sees her and jumps away from* KEITH *guiltily.*]

GRANDMA [*to* KEITH, *angrily*]: You can have the stew *she* were going to get tomorrow night! [*to* VIVIAN] *She's* getting sod-all in future, the little whore! [*She slams back into the kitchen.*]

VIVIAN [*horrified*]: I've buggered it!

KEITH: Buggered what?

VIVIAN: Don't you *know*???

KEITH: It'd be safer in your house. I'll come round tomorrow if you like.
> [VIVIAN *gazes at him, bathed in relief and happiness.*]

VIVIAN [*V.O.*]: 'If you like,' he said. Oh, brother! Did I like . . . !

33. Ext. Castleford main street. Day (1961).

[(*Note: In this scene and in Scenes 34, 35, 36 and 37, Vivian's hair is blue.*)
VIVIAN *is at the wheel of the parked Chevrolet. The car radio is playing.*
KEITH *approaches from down the street and gets in the car.*]

34. Int. Stationary Chevrolet. (Continuous in time.)

[KEITH *settles down in the passenger seat. He seems angry and upset.*
VIVIAN *looks at him.*]

VIVIAN: Well?
KEITH: Well what?
VIVIAN: Did you go to the bank?
KETIH: Are we sitting here all day?
VIVIAN [*irritated*]: Did you *go*?
KEITH: The snooty sods ... It's my brass isn't it? They treat me like arse-paper ... they laugh at me! It's my money – I can please myself *what* I do!
VIVIAN: Why – what did they say?
KEITH [*sighing unhappily, frustratedly*]: Usual double-dutch. Investment rate point how's-your-father per annum per capital pissholding per cent. I just let them get on with it ... I couldn't be bothered ...
[VIVIAN *starts the car. They drive off.*]

35. Ext. Grange Avenue. Day. Half-an-hour or so later.

[*As the Chevrolet, with* VIVIAN *and* KEITH *inside, draws up and stops outside* VIVIAN's *house, three men leap out of a parked car and run towards the Chevrolet.*]

36. Int. Parked Chevrolet, Grange Avenue.
(Continuous in time.)

[VIVIAN *and* KEITH *stare, terrified, at the three men racing towards them.*]

VIVIAN: Who are they??
KEITH: Christ knows!
VIVIAN: Keith – they're going to kill us!
KEITH: Lock your door!
   [*She does so. They both swiftly close their windows.*]
VIVIAN: Have they got guns?
   [*The three men have now arrived at the Chevrolet. They mouth and gesticulate at the windows.*]
   [*Hysterically*] What do they want???
   [KEITH *is beginning to understand their mouthings.*]
KEITH: Reporters. Sunday papers. *The People.*
VIVIAN: What do they want – for God's sake??

37. Int. Living room, Vivian's house, Grange Avenue.
The following Sunday morning.

VIVIAN [*V.O.*]: We found out on Sunday morning. So did the rest of the bloody world.
   [KEITH, *in pyjamas, enters from the stairs and picks up a copy of* The People, *dated 15 October 1961, which is lying on the mat. He starts flicking through it, worriedly.*
   VIVIAN, *in a frilly dressing gown, comes from the bedroom and joins him, scanning the pages, equally apprehensively.*
   They find what they're looking for.]
VIVIAN: Oh, God!
   [*They stand, reading the article.*]
MAN'S VOICE: 'Spending, spending, spending!! Keith Nicholson has been splashing his money about since he won £152,000 on the pools a few weeks ago. A brand-new

house, a shining American car, as much as they can drink for everyone at his local, and £10,000 on each of his children. [*Pause.*]. One child he's forgotten in this spend-ing-spree is a curly-haired, two-year-old toddler called Kim. *But I'm not going to let him forget.* I'm going to remind him that he's twenty-two pounds six shillings in arrears on payments which the local magistrates' court ordered him to pay for Kim's upkeep. [*Pause.*] Well, what about it, Keith? Twenty-five bob a week is a lot to people like the girl you jilted and the baby you left her with . . . or have you forgotten your own humble beginning so soon?'

    [*A pause.*]

VIVIAN: Decent photo of *me* . . .

MAN'S VOICE: 'And what about Keith's wife, former cinema-usherette, Vivian? All *she* said was "That woman isn't going to get a penny out of Keith if I can help it."'

VIVIAN [*unsure, to* KEITH]: *Did* I?

KEITH: He's not my kid! How many more times!

VIVIAN: You should've proved it at the time!

KEITH: How???

VIVIAN: Well, you'll have to put your hand in your pocket now, lad.

KEITH: I *am*! I'm paying! By banker's order!

VIVIAN [*not quite as confidently as she intends*]: It's only news-paper talk. No one takes notice of newspapers . . .

38. Ext. Grange Avenue. Day. (A few days later.)

[*Two* POLICEMEN *are patrolling up and down outside* VIVIAN'*s house, keeping guard.*
The Chevrolet, even dirtier than usual, is parked outside.
A POSTMAN *is going from house to house delivering the morning mail. He passes the* POLICEMEN *as he makes his way to* VIVIAN'*s front door.*]

POSTMAN: Morning.

FIRST P.C.: Morning.

POSTMAN: No one's blown their car up yet then?

FIRST P.C.: Not yet. They've had offers.

POSTMAN: I thought they'd have been blown up *themselves* by now.

FIRST P.C.: Give them time.

[*The* POSTMAN *laughs and starts dropping scores of letters through* VIVIAN's *letterbox.*
Close shot of the letterbox, as one by one, the letters are pushed through.
Over this, we hear:]

FIRST WOMAN'S VOICE: Dear Mrs Nicholson ... how would you feel if your stinking husband got strangled, then you? I'd enjoy seeing that.

FIRST MAN'S VOICE: I've read the paper, Nicholson. You're a heartless bastard, and your wife is a dirty whore. You want drowning, the pair of you ...

SECOND MAN'S VOICE: Watch out, Nicholson ... because *I'm* watching *you* ... and you're going to get a knife in your back. The police won't save you. And don't let your kids out because I'll murder them as well ...

39. Ext. The back yard, Matthew's house. Day (1954).

[*It's the morning after* VIVIAN's *first meeting with* KEITH *at his* GRANDMA's *house.*
The back door opens and VIVIAN *comes out of the house. She's ostensibly on her way to work but dressed as smartly as she can.*]

VIVIAN [*V.O.*]: 'I'll come round tomorrow,' Keith said. Well, this was it. This was tomorrow. They say tomorrow never comes. I kept my fingers crossed all night to make sure *that* bugger did! That morning, I left the house as per usual, making out to Matthew – and to any nosey bitches watching – that I was going to work.

[*She crosses the backyard and exits into the back alley.*]

40. Ext. Front street of Matthew's house.
    Day (A few hours later.)

VIVIAN [*V.O.*]: All I really did, though, was stay out a few hours – then come back the front way.
   [VIVIAN *appears from round the corner making her way to her front door, surreptitiously. She keeps herself as close to the wall as possible, so as not to be seen. She's not very good at it.*]
Creeping along like a Russian spy or summat, so's no one'd see me . . .
   [*She suddenly makes a mad dash for her front door, and puts the key in the lock. After a few moments of agonising trouble trying to turn the key, she finally lets herself in.*]

41. Int. Living room. Matthew's house.
    Evening of the same day.

[VIVIAN *is seated in an easy chair, agitatedly smoking a cigarette. It's dusk – but there are no lights on.*]

VIVIAN [*V.O.*]: I sat and sat and sat, while it grew dark. Not budging, so's the neighbours'd think I were still at work. Just waiting and twitching and smoking myself cross-eyed. I know lovers' meetings are supposed to be secret. But this were *too* secret. I mean, I was one of the lovers . . . and *I* didn't know what time it was going to happen! [*Pause.*] While I'd been out, I'd popped round to see my mother and baby Stephen. She was looking after him for me in them days. Well, I was busy working, wasn't I? [*defensively*] Well, not *that* day, granted. That day I was busy *panting* God. I was on heat . . . I'd taken my wedding-ring off and everything . . . Out of respect.
   [*Suddenly there's a barrage of knocking at the front door.*
   VIVIAN *jumps up startled, then excitedly races from the room.*]

42. Int. Hallway, Matthew's house.
(Continuous in time.)

[*The knocking at the front door continues.*
VIVIAN *races from the living room to the door.*]

VIVIAN [*half-to-herself*]: Not so loud, you turnip. [*Giggles.*]
Randy bugger . . . !
   [*She opens the front door.*
   MATTHEW *enters angrily.*
   VIVIAN'*s face falls in shock and bitter disappointment.*]
MATTHEW: I couldn't get my key in! [*He sees her key in the
inside lock.*] No bloody wonder! [*He pulls her key out.*]
You've left yours *in*! Have all the lights fused or summat?
What are you doing in the dark? [*He switches the hall-light
on.*]
VIVIAN: I had headache.
   [MATTHEW *tries to walk past her. She doesn't move aside.*
   He stares at her, puzzled.]
MATTHEW: Well, *shift*, then!
VIVIAN: Have you had your tea?
MATTHEW: Haven't you made me none?
VIVIAN: Go and have fish and chips.
MATTHEW: I don't *want* fish and chips.
VIVIAN: I'm expecting my mam round for a natter. I don't
want you under my feet.
MATTHEW: I bloody *live* here!
VIVIAN: Bloody scram or I'll fetch the police!
   [*He stands staring at her, at a loss.*]
MATTHEW: There's summat up, isn't there?
VIVIAN: I said scram!
MATTHEW: Do *you* want some?
VIVIAN: Some what?
MATTHEW: Fish and chips.
VIVIAN [*pushing him out of the door*]: Piss off out – and stay
out ! ! [*She slams the door after the departed* MATTHEW, *turns*

*the light off again, then leans her back against the door, panting
with relief.*] Is it worth it? Is it bloody worth it?

43. Ext. Vivian's house, Grange Avenue. Night (1961).

[*The lights are blazing from* VIVIAN's *living room. We hear the
record-player loudly playing, and sounds of a wild, drunken party in
progress.
A car drives up and stops in front of the parked Chevrolet. A*
DOCTOR *gets out, goes to the door of the house and rings the bell.
He has to ring several times to make himself heard above the noise.
Finally,* KEITH – *drink in hand and already drunk* – *opens the door
and admits him.*]

44. Int. Bedroom, Vivian's house, Grange Avenue.
(Continuous in time.)

[KEITH *leads the* DOCTOR *into the room.
The* DOCTOR *looks at the bed. From his P.O.V., we see a figure
lying on the bed . . . wearing horn-rimmed glasses, a false beard,
football jersey, socks and shorts. It's* VIVIAN . . . *very, very ill.*]

DOCTOR [*puzzled to* KEITH]: Where is she?
VIVIAN [*pulling her beard aside*]: Hi, Doc.
    [*The* DOCTOR *smiles then dismisses* KEITH.]
DOCTOR: All right, Mr Nicholson.
KEITH: Don't need me, do you? I'd only be in the way . . .
    [*He makes a rapid relieved exit.
The doctor approaches the bed.*]
DOCTOR: I like your costume.
VIVIAN: Sometimes I stick a banana out of the front. Any-
    thing for a laugh, that's me . . .
    [*She starts gently, helplessly crying.
The* DOCTOR *sits on the bed, patting her shoulder comfort-
ingly.*]

DOCTOR: Now what's the trouble, Mrs Nicholson, mm?

VIVIAN: Good question. I wish I knew.

DOCTOR: Tell me what's wrong.

VIVIAN: Shaking. Headaches. Can't breathe. I swell up all over. I just feel terrible. I keep thinking I'm going to die ... I can't think of nothing *else* ...

DOCTOR: Now why should you think you're going to die, eh?

VIVIAN: Because we won the money. It's punishment.

DOCTOR: Well, it'd be a nice change on certificates, wouldn't it? Cause of death – punishment. Come on, let's have a look at you, love ...

[*He starts examining her ... stethoscope, pulse, torch in her eyes etc. During this:*]

VIVIAN: I.can't get downstairs ... I have to shuffle on my backside. [*Pause.*] We're so *lonely*, doctor. No one wants to know us – unless it's to cadge a drink. No one invites us back. None of the neighbours speak. No 'Good morning', nothing, not a word. They make me feel ashamed of myself ... dirty ... ashamed of my family ... [*Pause.*] We spend hundreds of pounds at the Miners Arms on all our old mates. But they're not mates any more, really. Not now. They've nowt to talk to us about. So they don't. *No* one does. It's like everyone's a stranger. Or *we* are. [*Pause.*] I've no one to talk to. No one to listen ...

DOCTOR: I see. [*His examination is now completed.*] Well, I'll tell you what the trouble is.

VIVIAN: Punishment.

DOCTOR: You're in a state of shock.

VIVIAN: In what way?

DOCTOR: Shock. From winning the pools.

VIVIAN: Well, *I'll* tell *you* what the trouble is. If it's not punishment, it's the booze. It *must* be the booze. It's all I do! Day and night.

DOCTOR: Shock, that's all. State of shock. You haven't a thing to worry about, love.

45. Int. Living room, Matthew's house. Night.
The same night as Scene 42 (1954).

[VIVIAN *and* KEITH *are standing in the middle of the room,
kissing . . . very romantically, very passionately.*]

VIVIAN [*V.O.*]: 'Is it worth it?' I'll say it is! [*Pause.*] As
Matthew went out of the front door, Keith came in at the
back. We played cards for a bit, then . . . well, then we
just started kissing. [*Pause.*] Only kissing was kissing in
them days. Kissing was beautiful. My spine were doing
a jitterbug eight beats to the bar. [*Pause.*] I wanted to
ravish him, vampire him. To bite and scratch, to pull
him apart, to taste blood. It felt good. It felt right.
  [*We hear the back door opening.*
  KEITH *and* VIVIAN *spring apart.*]
VIVIAN [*terrified*]: You've never left the back door open!
KEITH: I didn't think.
VIVIAN: Quick! Upstairs!
  [*She pushes him into the hall just in time.*
  KEITH'S GRANDMA *bursts in from the kitchen door, sus-
  picious and looking for trouble.*]
[*V.O.*] You know what they say . . . If you're having a
pantomime, you need the Wicked frigging Witch . . .
GRANDMA: Where is he?
VIVIAN: Who?
GRANDMA: He's only a kid, you evil bastard!
VIVIAN: Who?
GRANDMA: I'll bloody find him! [*Storms past* VIVIAN *into
the hall.*]

46. Int. Matthew's house. Staircase.
(Continuous in time.)

[GRANDMA *enters from the living room and starts up the stairs.*
VIVIAN *enters from the living room, and starts running up the
stairs, pushing* GRANDMA *out of the way to race past her.*]

VIVIAN [*V.O.*]: As I got towards the bedroom, I heard the
window open . . .

47. Int. Bedroom, Matthew's house.
(Continuous in time.)

[KEITH *is at the open window. He jumps out.*
Cut to VIVIAN *at the door, watching, horrified.*
We hear KEITH *crash down to the pavement.*
GRANDMA *enters.*
VIVIAN *turns to her.*]

VIVIAN: See! No one. Satisfied?
[*V.O.*] All I could think was . . . if he's dead, that's my
sexual happening gone for a burton! And if he had've
been, I'll tell you summat else . . . *she'd* have been the
next on the list.

48. Int. Living room, Matthew's house.
(A few moments later.)

[GRANDMA *enters from upstairs and starts for the kitchen. She's
followed in by* VIVIAN.]

VIVIAN: Go on, get out, you evil sod!
GRANDMA: I'm sure he came in this house . . .
VIVIAN: Well, *you* won't again, baby!

GRANDMA: I wouldn't lower myself! Don't come in mine again neither! [*She starts for the kitchen.*]

VIVIAN [*suspiciously*]: Hey! I thought you were deaf?

GRANDMA [*immediately deaf again*]: You what?

[VIVIAN *ignores her.*

GRANDMA *exits.*

VIVIAN *stands, frightened, angry, frustrated. She suddenly picks up a cup from the table and smashes it against the wall.*]

VIVIAN [*V.O.*]: I were in such a temper, I could've killed *myself*! Got hold of my throat and throttled myself! [*Pause.*] She'd spoilt something so beautiful . . .

[*We hear the front door open, then close.* MATTHEW *enters from the hall.*]

MATTHEW: I didn't fancy fish and chips. I had steak pudding.

49. A montage series of photographs (1961).

[*A succession of holiday snaps, amateurishly framed, posed and shot, of* VIVIAN *and* KEITH *on holiday in Spain, Tangier and Gibraltar. They're wearing different holiday clothes in each of them (including one of* VIVIAN *in an extremely unflattering bikini). Most of the snaps are of* VIVIAN *and* KEITH *simply drinking at different bars, and grinning fatuously at the camera.*

Bright 'holiday' music of the period . . . over.]

VIVIAN [*V.O.*]: Before we won the pools, the furthest I'd ever been was the free Sunday School trip to Scarborough as a kid. Now here we were in Spain!

Keith had a blue fit when I told him I'd booked three weeks in Spain, Tangier and Gibraltar. He was homesick for a pint of Tetley's Mild the minute we got us passports. He cheered up when he found foreigners had booze as well. I got burnt to a frazzle every day, and drunk every night. *He* got drunk *day* and night. Compared to everyone else's, my bikini looked like summat the rag-and-bone man's dragged in. I don't know why. I bought it at Schofield's. And it's a class shop is Schofield's. One of the best in Leeds.

You know what foreign fellers are. All giving me the Glad Eye, the Oh-Be-Joyful. They said I were the spitting image of Brigitte Bardot. Not that I encouraged them. [*Pause.*] Not that Keith *believed* me. He thumped everyone in sight. Me included.

Tangier was worst. I mean, it's lovely – don't get me wrong – but there's poverty there you don't even see in Castleford. Skinny little kids living in caves. I gave them bars of chocolate. I mean there's poverty and poverty, isn't there? Keith liked Gibraltar best, because they sold English beer. Still, it was a good holiday all told. By the time we got back – I was ready for anyone . . .

50. Ext. Vivian's house, Grange Avenue. Day (1961).

[*The Chevrolet draws up opposite* VIVIAN's *front door.* VIVIAN *is very suntanned, and dressed in bright holiday clothes – sandals and sombrero. She stands looking around her, triumphantly. Suddenly, she cups her mouth with her hands, and starts yelling at all the surrounding houses, circling as she does so.*]

VIVIAN [*shouting*]: Well, where are you you pale-faced farts? All skenning through your curtains, are you? Your swanky, bloody curtains that aren't even paid for yet! Come out and fight, the lot of you! You sex-starved, lah-de-dah bastards!

    [*The street remains still and silent.* VIVIAN *drops her hands.* KEITH, *horrified, laden with luggage, stares at her.*]

KEITH: What are you showing yourself up for? ? ?

VIVIAN [*calmly*]: S'alright. I enjoyed it. The mood has passed.

    [*As* KEITH *lugs their brand-new suitcases towards their front door,* VIVIAN *suddenly stoops. Picks up a half-brick and hurls it through her next-door-neighbour's window. Immediately after we hear the sound of the crash of glass, cut to:*]

51. Ext. Vivian's bungalow, Garforth Cliffs. Day. (1962).

[*The Chevrolet is parked outside.*]

VIVIAN [*V.O.*]: . . . bang, wallop! We did a moonlight flit. The new bungalow were at Garforth Cliffs. It cost nine thousand and something. I had G-Plan furniture and everything . . . nothing but the best.

52. Int. Living room, Vivian's bungalow.
(Continuous in time.)

[*The room is vast. Alone, in the middle of it, sits* VIVIAN.]

VIVIAN [*V.O.*]: Everybody called it The Ponderosa. It was gorgeous . . . But I felt no different than I'd felt in Grange Avenue. No reason why I should really. I was still Vivian Nicholson, wasn't I? I were still bloody *me.*
  [*The phone rings, abruptly.*
  VIVIAN *jumps, startled, she grabs the phone.*]
Hello?
MAN'S VOICE: Mrs Nicholson?
VIVIAN: Yes. [*then, wary*] No! If you're an obscene call, you can sod off!
MAN'S VOICE: Castleford Police here, Mrs Nicholson.
VIVIAN [*resignedly*]: Oh, hell . . . Not Keith again?
MAN'S VOICE: Afraid so, love.
VIVIAN: Drunk again?
MAN'S VOICE: Just beginning to surface. He's had twelve cups of black coffee and the Riot Act.

VIVIAN: Shooting-brake buggered again?

MAN'S VOICE: Hard to tell, really. It's lying upside down waving its legs on the Huddersfield Road.

VIVIAN [*sighing wearily*]: Thanks, chuck. I'll come and fetch him. It's the most expensive Black Maria in Yorkshire, my Chevvy... [*She replaces the receiver.*]

53. Ext. Police station. An hour or so later.

[VIVIAN *is leaning against her Chevrolet, arms folded, wryly waiting for* KEITH. *He enters from the police station, dishevelled* ... *and troubled.*

VIVIAN *gets into the driver's seat.*

KEITH *turns to wave at a policeman who's followed him to the door of the police station, to wave him amicably off.* KEITH *gets into the passenger seat.*]

54. Int. Parked Chevrolet outside police station.
(Continuous in time.)

[VIVIAN *and* KEITH *in their seats.*]

VIVIAN: You've had a smashing time, then, I believe...

KEITH: I don't understand, Goldie...

VIVIAN: *I* do. You were pissed as a fart, driving along and...

KEITH [*very troubled, very grave*]: Not that.

VIVIAN: What don't you understand, then?

KEITH: Anything.

[*A troubled pause.*]

VIVIAN [*worried, quietly*]: In what way, cock?

KEITH: The days I had nowt, I'd borrow five bob off your mam – and I knew where I stood: I owed five bob. [*Pause.*] Now, when I've got hundred and fifty thousand quid...

VIVIAN: Nearer hundred thousand now, pet . . .

KEITH Hundred thousand then . . . and I've still got nowt! !
[*A pause.*]

VIVIAN: I don't follow, Keith . . .

KEITH: I went to the bank again. I wanted money for a
new shotgun and binoculars . . .

VIVIAN: You've got a shotgun and binoculars!

KEITH [*angrily*]: I want *new* 'uns! I'm a rich feller! I can
afford them! [*Pause. He calms down.*] I've ordered fresh
golf clubs, an' all. [*Pause.*] Anyroad, I called into the bank
for some money . . . and I got a bloody *lecture*. They make
me feel a bloody two-year-old! They make me feel guilty
. . . [*Mimics bank manager's educated accents.*] 'You're three
thousand overdrawn, Mr Nicholson. You've burnt all
your tax demands again, haven't you, Mr Nicholson?
Instead of spending, take up a hobby, Mr Nicholson.'
[*Shouting, angrily, as himself.*] Spending is my bloody
hobby! ! !
[*A pause.*]

VIVIAN [*tentatively*]: The Littlewoods feller always advised
us to . . .

KEITH [*angrily*]: 'Advised'? Nagged, you mean! That
weren't advising, that were nagging! [*Pause.*] [*Quietly*]
I'm a very wealthy chap . . . and they make me feel as
though I'm applying for National Assistance. [*To* VIVIAN,
helplessly] Now how is that humanly possible, with my
own brass? I don't follow neither . . .

VIVIAN [*glumly*]: Makes two of us . . .
[*A pause.*]

KEITH [*sighing*]: Anyroad, I'm going to buy some fishing
tackle tomorrow. Best money can buy . . .

55. Int. 'Kiosk' dance hall. Evening (1956).

[*The spinning silver ball in the centre of the ceiling is spinning.*
Couples are dancing. Dance music playing.
Over this, we hear:]

VIVIAN [*V.O.*]: Matthew came home from work with his
pit boots on – and trod on my toes. He said it were
accidental. I forgave him – but my toes didn't. Four of
them was broken. They swelled up like half a pound of
Walls Pork and Beef. The hospital put them in plaster
and said I'd to keep off my feet for a month.
  [*Close up of* VIVIAN's *feet as she dances. Her feet and shoes*
  look as described below.]
Then they got septic, throbbing and huge and festering.
So I boiled some water and the end of a knife, shut my
eyes and stabbed them. All the septic white pus flew all
over the room – but I was cured. I bathed my feet in
Dettol and hot water, cut the toecaps off my shoes,
bandaged my toes . . . and went dancing.
  [*Pan up the legs and body of* VIVIAN *and her partner as they*
  dance. We now see that she's dancing with KEITH.]
There was method in my madness . . . I knew *Keith'd* be
there!
  [VIVIAN *and* KEITH *are dancing very close together and*
  with increasing passion.
  MATTHEW *stands with spectators at the edge of the dance*
  floor, eyeing them both with bitter suspicion.]
I don't think Matthew trusted us.

56. Ext. Canalside. Night. A few hours later.

VIVIAN [*V.O.*]: I expect he had his reasons . . .
  [*Beneath a bridge, among lumps of coal and cinders and over-*
  grown weeds, we see KEITH *and* VIVIAN *tearing each*
  other's clothes off with mounting passion.]

Keith told me how many light years the stars were from the earth. But I wasn't listening. It's a hell of a lot, though.
[*They begin to make love. Pale, shadowy, naked figures in the moonlight.*]
It were freezing that night. But we weren't. Only our noses. [*Pause.*] It was the greatest sexual happening in the history of Castleford. In the history of the world.

57. Ext. Field. Later the same night.

[VIVIAN *and* KEITH *on the ground, making love.*]
VIVIAN [*V.O.*]: Then we did it again. And again. And again. And again. And again. Bare skin against my lips. Bare skin on *my* skin ... Then bare skin on a nest of bloody ants!!
[VIVIAN *leaps up, holding her ant-bitten buttocks.* KEITH'*s laughing. She's screaming.*]

58. Int. Hospital ward. Day (1957).

[*Close-up of* VIVIAN *screaming – she is in labour.*]

VIVIAN [*V.O.*]: After that night, I didn't see Keith for over nine months. Till after his daughter was born. Our Susan. He knew I was pregnant – but his grandma convinced him he wasn't the father ... And he seemed happy enough to believe her. I thought 'I'll have to get the poor bugger adopted. I've no option ...'

59. Int. Vivian's parents' back room, Kershaw Avenue (1957).

[MOTHER, DAD *and* VIVIAN, *all seated, finishing mugs of tea.* VIVIAN *holds baby Susan in her arms: her* MOTHER *holds the infant Stephen on her knee.*]

VIVIAN [*V.O.*]: When I left hospital, I went to see my mam in her new council house in Kershaw Avenue . . .

[*They all sit in troubled silence.*]

DAD: She's your child – you bloody look after her! Any more talk of adoption, and I'll kick your teeth so far down your throat you'll be spitting them out of your arse!

[*A pause.*]

VIVIAN [*helplessly, quietly, near to tears*]: I can't *afford* to . . . She'll starve. All I've got is three pounds and a shilling from the National Assistance. Three pound one, and a butter token . . .

[*A pause.*]

DAD [*quietly*]: You can go back to Matthew.

VIVIAN: I can hell-as-like.

MOTHER: What about the father?

VIVIAN: He doesn't want to know. He's got nowt. I'm asking him for nowt. There's such a thing as self-respect.

MOTHER: She can stay here then. The two of you. [*She notices Stephen on her knee, and sighs.*] The three of you.

VIVIAN: You've enough with your own!

MOTHER: I'll have a bit more then, won't I . . .?

VIVIAN [*bathed in relief*]: I'll clean for you, Mam! I'll earn my board, honest!

DAD: Too true you will! You can tip up your Lloyd George money for a kick-off!

VIVIAN: Aye, aye! Beer and Woodbines calling, are they?

[DAD *hits her across the head.*

They sit there in silence.]

VIVIAN [*V.O.*]: Well . . . there's worse things at sea, isn't there? What's two kids, no husband, no money and no home? Nothing. So I cadged an old skirt off our Jessie, and a jumper and a pair of shoes . . . and I carried on where I'd left off . . .

60. Int. 'Kiosk' dance hall. Night (1957).

[KEITH *is standing on the edge of the dance-floor, self-consciously puffing an unaccustomed pipe.*
VIVIAN *and her girlfriend dance by.*
KEITH's *and* VIVIAN's *eyes meet momentarily, then they both look away again.*]

VIVIAN [*V.O.*]: Keith was there, puffing away at a pipe that kept going out. I played it cool when I saw him. Hard to get. I played it cool for – oh – nearly twenty minutes . . .

61. Ext. Canalside. Night, an hour or so later.

[VIVIAN *and* KEITH *kissing passionately beneath the bridge.*]

VIVIAN [*V.O.*] He told me he'd tried to come and see me in hospital – but they wouldn't let him in. 'Well,' I thought, 'sod it. Forgive and forget.'

62. A montage of different close-shots of Keith and Vivian making love (1957).

VIVIAN [*V.O.*]: I forgave and forgot down back-alleys, on railway sidings, under canal bridges, on the allotments, on the kitchen floor when his grandma was in bed. I forgave and forgot wherever we could get our clouts off without no one seeing. [*Pause.*] I was so busy forgiving, I forgot summat *else*: that that's where babies come from.

63. Int. Kitchen, Parents' house, Kershaw Avenue. Day (1957).

[VIVIAN *sits at the table, with baby Susan in her arms and Stephen in his high chair beside her. She's surveying a mass of pill-boxes and bottles on the table.*]

VIVIAN [*V.O.*]: I was in the pudding club again, wasn't I? I tried everything: gin, quinine, mustard baths, magnetic potash, lemonade and epsom salts. I had the lot.

64. Ext. Grandma's back yard. Day (1958).

[VIVIAN *enters from the back alley. She carries a bundle of belongings and baby Tim in a makeshift cradle.*]

VIVIAN [*V.O.*]: And the next thing I had was the *baby*. [*Pause.*] Premature, jaundiced, three pounds in weight. We called him Tim. And he slept in a Timpson's shoe-box.
    [GRANDMA *stands at her back door, wryly watching* VIVIAN *cross the yard towards her.*]
VIVIAN [*V.O.*]: Naturally, me mam chucked me and Tim out. She'd enough on her plate with my other two. And Matthew divorced me. For adultery, I believe. So Keith's grandma said we could live there . . . with her and Keith. [*Pause.*] The old sod was in her element. Crowing. Not like a *crow*, mind you. Like a bleeding vulture.
    [VIVIAN *smiles at her sarcastically.*
    GRANDMA *smiles sarcastically back.*
    C.U. VIVIAN *smiling.*]
Do you like a good laugh? Well, wait for it . . . Tim was eight weeks old at the time . . . and I was pregnant again.

65. A montage series of postcards (1964).

[*Postcards from* VIVIAN *and* KEITH *on holiday. This time in the
United States.
Music over:* ('*I Wanna be in America*' *from* West Side Story.]

VIVIAN [*V.O.*]: Keith had another blue fit – so did the
bank manager – when I booked a month's holiday in
America.
The best thing about Los Angeles was Disneyland. The
worst thing was the taxi-drivers. The only thing they
knew about England was the Beatles. They hated them
because their girl-friends loved them.
We got to Dallas exactly a year after President Kennedy
got shot. I had to go ... I thought a lot of President
Kennedy. It was a right rough hole, was Dallas. I'm
surprised there's anyone left who *hasn't* got shot.
In New York I learnt to cut steak up with my knife, then
eat it just with the fork. I always eat like that now. The
food were very nice, but I don't think they've ever heard
of vegetables ... sprouts or a nice cauli. They haven't
invented them yet.
I saw real colour telly there an' all. It stays on till God-
knows-what time ... so we never got much sleep. I mean,
you have to watch it to the end, haven't you, or you don't
know what happens ...
New York was very clean ... but there's no night life.
Everything closes at midnight. You get a livelier night
out in Castleford. Still, it was America ... and we went.
I mean, it's a dream in people's minds, isn't it, going to
America?

66. Int. Bungalow bedroom. Day (1964).

VIVIAN [*V.O.*]: Coming home was a nightmare.

[*It's about 8 a.m.* VIVIAN *and* KEITH *are in separate beds.*
KEITH *is sipping a cup of tea and reading the* Daily Mirror.
VIVIAN's *tea is untouched and cold at the bedside. She's lonely
and unhappy. She starts quietly to weep.*
KEITH *shoots her an irritated glance.*]

KEITH: What's up with you, then?

VIVIAN: Bit of a cold, that's all.

[KEITH *returns to his paper. He starts singing to himself. He
glances at his watch.*]

KEITH: Bloody hell! Ten past!

[*He jumps out of bed and starts taking his pyjamas off to dress.*
VIVIAN *watches him, coldly, emptily.*]

VIVIAN: Where is it today, then? Horse-racing or shooting?
[*No reply.*] Horse-racing or fishing? [*No reply.*] Horse-
racing or smashing your car up? [*No reply.*] Horse-racing
or horse-racing? [*No reply.*] Why don't you try boozing for
a change?

KEITH [*angrily*]: Say the word and you can have a crack
across the jaw. Just say the word.

VIVIAN: Go on, sod off with your racing pals!

KEITH: You can't stand decent people, can you? Folk with
a bob or two and a bit of bloody breeding!

VIVIAN: Oh I love them! Specially their fifty-year-old
wives, stripping off when they've got two Babychams
inside them and wiggling their fifty-year-old tits!

[KEITH *hits her hard.*]

[*V.O.*] He was good at that, was Keith. I think he went
to the same university as my dad.

[KEITH *is rapidly, angrily dressing.*]

KEITH [*bitterly*]: Why aren't you happy!

VIVIAN: Why aren't *you*!! [*She watches him dress in silence.
Tears well up in her eyes again.*] [*Gently, vulnerably*] Would
you like to come in bed with me for a few minutes?

[*He ignores her.*]

[*Bitterly*] Or have you forgotten the bloody password!

KEITH: I've to be at Beverley Races by twelve.

[*Emptily,* VIVIAN *watches him dress. She reaches for a cigarette and lights it.*]

VIVIAN [*V.O.*]: I thought of having an affair. An orgy. A dozen orgies. [*Pause.*] You can't, though, really, can you? Not when you love someone . . .

67. Int. Vivian's living room, Kershaw Avenue (1961).

[*Much of the room is newly, but cheaply furnished.*
KEITH, *just home from his shift, wearing his pit clothes and helmet and unwashed, is seated at the table, concentrating on his pools coupon, pen at the ready.*]

VIVIAN [*V.O.*]: After me and Keith were married, my mother got us a council house on Kershaw Avenue – the same street as her – a few doors down. We paid 38 shillings rent, seven and six a week for the telly, another seven and six HP, and carpet and standard lamp – ten bob. Keith also forked out thirty bob a week for a baby called Kim who he were reckoned to be the father to.

68. Int. Vivian's kitchen, Kershaw Avenue.
(Continuous in time.)

[VIVIAN, *tired out, washed out, wearing threadbare work-clothes, and carrying a shopping bag, comes in from work.*]

VIVIAN [*V.O.*]: And it all came out of Keith's seven quid a week, and the tuppence ha'penny a week I earned at Ewbank's Sweet Factory.
    [VIVIAN *calls towards living room.*]
It's only me!

69. Int. Vivian's living room, Kershaw Avenue.
(Continuous in time.)

[KEITH *is poring over his pools coupon.*
VIVIAN *enters from kitchen.*
KEITH *ignores her.*]

VIVIAN [*V.O.*]: Our life savings amounted to six quid –
and I was saving that up for some glass doors for the
front room. You know, modernizing . . .
[VIVIAN *looks round, furiously.*]
Well, where are they!!

KEITH [*concentrating on his coupon*]: Who?

VIVIAN: 'Who??' The bloody kids! There's four snotty-
nosed kids live here! You must've noticed the scabby sods!

KEITH [*unruffled, still concentrating*]: I thought you were
picking them up from your mam's.

VIVIAN: I've been grafting all day!

KEITH: So have I.

VIVIAN: Aye. At bloody pontoon! [*She starts angrily for the
kitchen.*]

KEITH: Goldie – pick a number.

VIVIAN [*stopping*]: You what??

KEITH: Shout out eight numbers. Any'll do.
[VIVIAN *stares at him in angry incredulity.*]

VIVIAN: Not the bloody pools again!

KEITH: 'Again'?

VIVIAN: You've tried the pools *before*!

KEITH: Three times. That's nothing.

VIVIAN: It's five bloody *bob*! Do you know what five bob
is! Five bob's two loaves of bread and half a pound of
sodding butter!

KEITH: Shout out eight numbers.

VIVIAN [*starting to exit again*]: Sod off!

KEITH: Goldie!!

VIVIAN: One, two, three, four, five, six, seven, eight.
KEITH [*calling after her*]: Don't act so bloody gormless!

70. Int. Vivian's kitchen, Kershaw Avenue.
(Continuous in time.)

[VIVIAN *storms in from the living room, to make her way to the back door.*
Intercut, as required, to KEITH *in the living room, marking his coupon according to* VIVIAN'S *numbers.*]

VIVIAN: Eleven, twenty-two, thirty-seven . . .
KEITH: Hang on! Hang on!
VIVIAN: Five, one, forty-three and fifty-three.
KEITH: One more!
VIVIAN: Fifty-four. [*She slams out of the door.*]

71. Ext. Back-entry of Kershaw Avenue. Day.
(Continuous in time.)

[VIVIAN, *carrying her shopping bag, is striding miserably, angrily, towards her parents' house.*]

VIVIAN [*V.O.*]: I just couldn't see no future for any of us. How life could ever be any different. They say hard work never killed no one. Hunger has, though. *Hunger* and hard work. I mean, would they let a mother and four kids actually starve to death? In England? In 1961?
That week, the day after payday, I had eightpence in my purse. I went into Tesco's and pinched half a pound of Lurpak and a quarter of Typhoo tea. I bought a tin of first-aid-plasters with the eightpence.
[VIVIAN *enters her parents' backyard.*]

72. Int. Kitchen, Parents' house, Kershaw Avenue.
(Continuous in time.)

[VIVIAN *enters quietly and closes the door behind her. O.O.V.,
in the living room, we hear her parents violently arguing and the four
kids crying. She stands for a moment, listening.
She notices a baby's plate on the high chair. The plate is smeared
with congealed gravy. She picks up the plate and licks the gravy off.
She takes a partially-eaten slice of bread from the table and some
leftover mashed potato from a plate in the sink, and makes a sandwich. While eating the sandwich she silently steals tins of food from
the cupboards. She throws the tins into her shopping-bag.*]

VIVIAN [*V.O.*]: I never felt guilty pinching from my mother.
My dad had pinched *my* rent money from the cocoa tin
often enough. Forty-eight quids-worth once. It took him
two days to drink it, and ten minutes to spew it back.
[MOTHER *enters and jumps in surprise.*]
MOTHER: How long have *you* been in?
VIVIAN: Just now.
[MOTHER *gives her a dirty look.*]
What's up with your fizzog?
MOTHER: You're not fair, our Vivian. You should have
been here half an hour ago. It's too big a handful, four
of them . . . My head's . . .
VIVIAN: I had to get Keith his tea.
MOTHER [*doubtingly*]: Have *you* had?
VIVIAN: What?
MOTHER: Your tea.
VIVIAN: I had a big dinner.
MOTHER: What did you have?
VIVIAN: It's like the third degree in this house!
MOTHER: You owe me five bob, by the way.
[VIVIAN *stares at her, horrified.*]
VIVIAN: I what???
MOTHER: Keith borrowed it for his postal order.

VIVIAN: I'm not with you.

MOTHER: His pools.

VIVIAN: I haven't *got* five bob!!

[*The kids' crying O.O.V. reaches a crescendo.*]

MOTHER: Will you go and get them! They're *your* kids!

[VIVIAN *freezes, stares at her, fearing the worst.*]

VIVIAN: What's that supposed to mean?

MOTHER: I've had enough. I don't want them back.

VIVIAN: Tomorrow, you mean?

MOTHER: Tomorrow, the day after, the day after that. Ever again.

[*Blind with rage,* VIVIAN *takes two half-crowns from her purse and slings them at her* MOTHER.]

VIVIAN: There's your five bob! Stick it in your burial club!!

73. Ext. Kershaw Avenue. A few minutes later.

[VIVIAN *emerges from the front door of her parents' house. She carries her shopping bag and baby Howard, and pushes Tim, Susan and Stephen along in front of her. She makes her way down the street, angrily pushing the dawdling kids.*]

VIVIAN [*V.O.*]: Well, that were it! With no one to mind the kids, I'd have to give up my job. And without my wage coming in, we'd had it. [*Pause.*] If I'd had a shilling for the gas, I'd have stuck my head in the oven and got my money's worth . . .

74. Int. Vivian's living room, Kershaw Avenue.
The following Saturday (1961) Day.

[KEITH, *in his shirtsleeves, is shaving at the mirror over the mantelpiece, with soap, brush and razor.*
VIVIAN *is putting on a pair of nylons.*
The TV set is on.]

VIVIAN [*V.O.*]: The following Saturday, four quid – out of the six I'd saved up – went when the TV chap called for his arrears. So I thought 'Sod it!', I thought. I cadged a pair of nylons and a pair of shoes from our Jessie, and organized my dad to babysit for ten bob, while me and Keith blew the rest in the Miners Arms. Thirty bob might not be much to Tetley's Brewery – but it was all we had left in the world ... They could have the bastard!

TV ANNOUNCER: Now here are today's football results...

[VIVIAN *makes a hole in her nylons.*]

VIVIAN: Damn!

KEITH: Shurrup, will you!

TV ANNOUNCER: English League Division One. Arsenal 1, Birmingham City 1.

KEITH [*peering calmly at his copy coupon, while shaving*]: Fair start. We've got that bugger.

75. A blank screen.

[*We hear a screaming, frightening screech of brakes – followed by a very violent crash.*]

76. Ext. Country road. Day (1964).

[KEITH'S *car is lying at a drunken angle, wheels still spinning, engine billowing smoke.*
Zoom very, very slowly during the following voice-over to the corpse in the driving seat.]

B

VIVIAN [*V.O.*]: On his way back from Beverley Races, Keith had a crash. I had one myself the same day. I ran into a Mini that was parked in the road. There was a couple on the back seat, bollock-bare, bang in the middle of a sexual happening ...
When I got home, there were four policemen waiting for

me. I thought 'Now for it. They want to take my licence off me.' But they didn't.

They'd come to tell me about Keith's crash.

[*The zoom ends in a C.U. of the corpse twisted awkwardly in his seat. It's* KEITH. *His eyes are open and staring, his shirt is drenched in blood. Blood runs from his mouth down his chin.*]

One of the policemen started crying. 'Is it bad?' I said. 'Yes,' he said, 'it is, love. He's dead.'

77. Int. Vivian's living room, Kershaw Avenue. Day (1961).

[*As before.* KEITH *shaving while checking his coupon;* VIVIAN *dressing.*]

TV ANNOUNCER: Chelsea 1, Blackburn Rovers 1.

KEITH [*mildly amused*]: Got that bugger an' all! [*He cuts himself shaving.*] Ow!

78. Int. Vivian's living room, Garforth Estate. Evening (1964).

[VIVIAN *is alone in the vast living room. She sits motionless, staring blankly into space, a drink in her hand.*]

VIVIAN [*V.O.*]: The police took away Keith's shotguns in case I tried to do myself in. The doctor gave me five sleeping pills and two injections. [*Pause.*] Who was going to love me now? All I could think was 'Who's going to love me now...?'

79. Int. Vivian's living room, Kershaw Avenue.
Day (1961).

[KEITH *and* VIVIAN *as before.* KEITH *shaving. The cut on his throat is now bleeding quite steadily.*]

TV ANNOUNCER: Wolverhampton Wanderers 1, Cardiff
   City 1.
   [KEITH *quite pleased with his little self.*]
KEITH: Hey ... We've three up, love ... three out of
   three so far ...
   [VIVIAN *ignores him.*]
TV ANNOUNCER: League Division Two ...

80. Int. Vivian's living room, Garforth Estate.
Day. (1964)

[*The room is thickly crowded with* VIVIAN'*s parents, brothers, sisters, the four kids, Littlewoods Pools representatives, friends, neighbours all chatting among themselves, and munching sandwiches.* VIVIAN *stands to one side, alone, watching them.*]

VIVIAN [*V.O.*]: The funeral was beautiful. And the police
   were fantastic. They stopped all the traffic on the way to
   the cemetery. It was like royalty. And there were
   thousands there – friends from the old days – everybody
   we'd ever known. [*A beat.*] And I haven't seen one of
   them since ... from that day to this. [*Pause.*] That night,
   burglars broke in and pinched whatever they could lay
   hands on.

81. Int. Vivian's living room, Kershaw Avenue. Day (1961).

[KEITH *is absently dabbing his handkerchief against his bleeding cut, while checking his coupon.* VIVIAN *is still dressing.*]

TV ANNOUNCER: Stoke City 3, Norwich City 1 ... Sunderland 4, Scunthorpe United nil ...
KEITH [*to himself*]: It's this next 'un we want ...
TV ANNOUNCER: Swansea Town 3 ...
KEITH [*disappointed*]: Oh, hell!
TV ANNOUNCER: Middlesbrough 3.
KEITH [*grinning*]: Got another, Goldie!
VIVIAN [*fed up, sarcastic*]: Hip, hip, hoo-bloody-ray.

82. Int. Travelling Chevrolet. Day (1964).

[VIVIAN *is driving at a frightening speed. She's drunk and crying. She starts screaming again and again at the top of her voice. Through the screams we hear:*]

VIVIAN [*V.O.: simply, calmly, matter-of-fact*]: I drank harder than ever. I was never sober. I never changed my clothes. I never had a bath. I never changed the bedding ... I kept looking under the pillows to see if there was one ... just one ... of Keith's eyelashes. There was nothing.

83. Int. Vivian's living room, Kershaw Avenue. Day (1961).

[KEITH *and* VIVIAN *as before.* KEITH'S *chin, throat and shirt are now much more bloodied.*]

TV ANNOUNCER: Coventry 1, Peterborough 3.

KEITH: Next one we want is Grimsby.

TV ANNOUNCER: Crystal Palace 1, Portsmouth 2.

VIVIAN [*glancing at him*]: You know you've blood on your only bloody shirt, don't you!

TV ANNOUNCER: Grimsby Town 1, Port Vale 1.

KEITH: Hey up! Five out of five!

VIVIAN [*looking in a drawer*]: There's some plasters somewhere. I bought a tin in the week. Eightpence.

84. Int. Vivian's living room, Garforth Estate. Night (1964).

[*It's night. The living room is in darkness.*
VIVIAN *sits by the phone, drink in hand, staring into space.*]

VIVIAN [*V.O.*]: I used to sit by the phone like a zombie, thinking Keith might phone. Thinking ... even though he's dead, he might just phone me ...

   [*The phone rings.*
   She picks up the receiver.]

Garforth 2719.

MAN'S VOICE: Hello, Goldie.

VIVIAN [*V.O.*]: Keith was the only one in the world who ever called me Goldie.

VIVIAN [*terrified, into phone*]: Who's that???

MAN'S VOICE: Fancy coming out with me tonight, Goldie?

VIVIAN [*screaming into phone*]: Who is it!!!

   [*The phone clicks off.*
   She stares at the dead receiver.]

85. Int. Vivian's living room, Kershaw Avenue. Day (1961).

[KEITH *is now bleeding profusely.*

VIVIAN *is applying lipstick to her lips.*]

TV ANNOUNCER: Watford 3, Queen's Park Rangers 2.

KEITH: Next one we want's 37 . . . Darlington v. Bradford.

TV ANNOUNCER: League Division Four. Accrington Stanley nil, Aldershot 2.

KEITH: [*re-checking previous results*]: We've got all of them so far. Five out of five . . .

TV ANNOUNCER: Chesterfield nil, Mansfield Town 4.

KEITH: Come on, sweethearts!

TV ANNOUNCER: Darlington 3 . . .

KEITH [*face falling*]: We've had it!

TV ANNOUNCER: Bradford City 3.

KEITH [*trembling, hoarse*]: Christ. That's six, Goldie . . . We've got six out of six . . .

> [*For the first time* VIVIAN *takes a tense interest in what's happening. As the* TV ANNOUNCER *continues, she goes to* KEITH, *slowly, gravely, apprehensively.*]

TV ANNOUNCER: Doncaster Rovers 3, Crewe Alexandra nil. Gillingham 3, Millwall 1. Hartlepools United nil, Carlisle United 3 . . .

VIVIAN [*scared, nervous*]: Which do we want next?

KEITH [*tensely*]: Shurrup!! Oldham.

TV ANNOUNCER: Oldham Athletic nil, Stockport County nil.

> [*They stare at each other, hardly daring to breathe.*]

KEITH: Christ!

VIVIAN: Christ Almighty . . . Seven?

> [KEITH *is trembling violently. He tries to speak as quietly and calmly as possible.*]

KEITH: We've won a few bob here . . . happen hundred quid . . . Go and get your dad . . . He can check them again with me . . . Goldie! Get your sodding dad! Tell him we've seven draws . . .

> [*Meanwhile, the* TV ANNOUNCER *has continued giving the results of Division Four and started on the Scottish League, Division One.*

VIVIAN *bolts for the door. As she reaches it*:]
We've only one more to go ... St Johnstone ... Number
54 ... St Johnstone ...
TV ANNOUNCER: St Johnstone 1 ...
[VIVIAN *stops.*
They stand staring numbly at each other.]
Motherwell 1.
[*A long, staring pause.*
The TV ANNOUNCER *continues with the results, But*
KEITH *and* VIVIAN *are no longer listening.*]
KEITH [*quiet, trembling*]: Eight. Eight draws up. Goldie,
we've won the bastard. We've won the pools. Us. We've
won ... [*His throat and shirt are drenched in blood.*]

86. Int. Vivian's living room, Garforth Estate.
Day (1964).

[VIVIAN *stands alone.*
The room is now much denuded of furniture.]

VIVIAN [*V.O.*]: Remember Vivian Nicholson with hundred
and fifty thousand pounds to spend? I was broke.
The bank barged in and took everything ... even the
ten quid he had in his wallet when he died. The tax people
did the same. They looked under the bed, in drawers, in
the wash-house. They said the car, the bungalow – everything we possessed – belonged to the estate. Nothing
belonged to *me*. They said don't bother contesting it. But
I did. It took six years.

87. Int. Vivian's living room, Kershaw Avenue.
Day (1961).

[*It's the Monday after the Saturday pools win of Scene 85.*
KEITH *is seated at the table, literally crying with frustration.*

MOTHER, DAD *and* VIVIAN *are eating chip butties and drinking beer. The three of them are giving* KEITH *hostile, suspicious, angry looks.*]

VIVIAN [*V.O.*]: Saturday night we borrowed five quid off my mother and got drunk. Sunday, believe it or not, we found a pound note in the street and got drunk again. By Monday, we thought the eight draws must be a mistake. All in the mind, sort of style . . .

KEITH: Look, we checked the bloody coupon, didn't we!!

MOTHER: What if you filled it in wrong! What if what you sent in was different!

KEITH: It wasn't!

DAD: And you're sure you posted it?

KEITH: I posted it! I posted it! I filled it in, filled in the copy, sent the claims-telegram, checked the copy — I've done everything! Everybody says we've won. The whole street. Everyone I talk to . . .

VIVIAN: Everyone bar Littlewoods.

[*A pause.*
They all sit morosely. They've been through the same arguments for two days now.]

KEITH: If it's 75,000 quid, what room can we stack it in?

VIVIAN: You haven't bloody won it!

KEITH [*ignoring her*]: What if we haven't a room big enough?

DAD: They don't give it you in ones. It's in fivers.

KEITH: Or tenners.

DAD: What tenners?

KEITH: Ten pound notes.

DAD: There's no such thing.

KEITH: There was a feller in the Miners Arms had one . . .

[*A pause.*
They drink, make butties out of their chips.]

MOTHER [*grimly*]: Well, I'll tell you what *I* think.

DAD: Do you bloody *have* to?

MOTHER [*to* VIVIAN, *with certainty and finality*]: He never sent the bugger. He never sent the pools off. He never

sent a postal order. He cadged the five bob off me for it —
then spent it. He's won *nowt*.

KEITH: Oh, give me strength . . .

MOTHER [*to* VIVIAN]: Your dad's been doing it donkey's
years. Week in, week out. 'I think I've got eight draws
up, love. Lend me ten bob till my money comes through.'
All his life.

[VIVIAN *leaps up, crying tears of anger. She smashes her
plate down.*]

VIVIAN [*to* KEITH]: Bastard!

KEITH: She's talking about *him*!

VIVIAN [*to* KEITH]: Bastard!

DAD [*angrily to* KEITH]: Is that what you did?

KEITH: No! I keep telling you no!

VIVIAN [*to* KEITH]: Stinking bastard! [*She rushes into the
kitchen.*]

88. Int. Kitchen, Kershaw Avenue.
(Continuous in time.)

[VIVIAN *races in, and hysterically starts smashing all the crockery
within reach.*]

89. Int. Vivian's living room, Kershaw Avenue.
(Continuous in time.)

[KEITH, MOTHER, FATHER, *as before.
We hear knocking at the front door.*]

DAD: Is that someone at the door?
[*All three look at each other.
DAD gets up and exits to hall.
KEITH tries to get there first.*]

90. Int. Vivian's hallway, Kershaw Avenue.
(Continuous in time.)

[*The knocking continues.*
DAD enters from the living room and opens the front door.
A MAN is standing on the step.]

MAN: Mr Nicholson? Keith Nicholson?
DAD: I'm his father-in-law. I think it'll be me you want.
  [KEITH *and* VIVIAN *come racing down the hallway from
  the living room.*]
KEITH: Who is it?
VIVIAN: Who is it, dad?
  [DAD *puts his arm out to stop them reaching the door.*]
DAD: I'll deal with it.
MAN [*to* KEITH]: Mr Keith Nicholson?
KEITH: I'm Keith Nicholson.
VIVIAN: He is, yes. Mr Keith Nicholson.
DAD: It'll be *me* you want, though . . .
  [KEITH *knocks* DAD's *arm out of the way.*]
KEITH [*to the man*]: What is it?
MAN: Good afternoon, Mr Nicholson. I'm from Littlewoods
  Pools.

91. Int. Strip club. Night (1967).

[*A tinselly, tatty strip club.*
A sparse, uninterested male audience.
On stage, VIVIAN *is singing, wearing only bra and panties. On
either side of her are two strippers slowly stripping.*
Members of the audience jeer and leer half-heartedly.
The song VIVIAN *is singing is 'Hey, Big Spender!'.*]

VIVIAN [*V.O.*]: Life's been a barrel of laughs since Keith
  died . . . I did the car in a few hundred times. I tried to

do *myself* in once. My mam died, coughing her socks off
... and I met a lad called Brian. Met him, married him
and divorced him ... all in thirteen weeks. And out of
them I only lived with him for four days. A *busy* four days,
though: he broke my jaw, split my head open, stubbed
his cigarette out on my lip, and dropped a vase on my
head from the top of the stairs. I had to sign myself into
a mental home to escape.

Brian got killed in a car crash as well. Of course, lucky
bugger me, I wasn't eligible for widow's pension because
he didn't have the sense to kill himself till after the
divorce came through.

I was so broke, I got this lousy job in a lousy Manchester
strip club. I didn't want to sing that song. That's one
song I never wanted to sing ...

92. Newspaper cuttings: *The People* throughout
September 1970.

VIVIAN [*V.O.*]: I got 20,000 quid from Keith's estate after
contesting it. And I blew the lot.

I went to Malta to start a new life. Two weeks and four
thousand pound later, I got kicked out ... thanks to the
English Sunday papers. Deported. For offending the
Pope – which I didn't; threatening to open a strip joint –
which I didn't; and thumping a policeman – which I
did.

You remember Mr Mintoff chucking the British troops
out? I got blamed for that an' all.

93. Int. Strip club. Night (1967).

[*As scene 91:* VIVIAN *still singing her song, the strippers still
stripping.*]

VIVIAN [*V.O.*]: I toured the clubs, singing. I opened a boutique, sold everything at cost price, and closed the bugger again – penniless. I chased the bailiffs out with a broom, and the tax-inspector with Keith's old twelve-bore shotgun.

My dad died ... and went to the Great Tetley's Brewery in the Sky. After his funeral, I got arrested for being drunk and disorderly. He'd have liked that.

And I married a lad called Graham. The highspot of the marriage was a packet of crisps for our wedding breakfast. *That* marriage lasted a week. *We* hated every minute. The newspapers *loved* every minute.

94. Int. Gary's living room. Evening (1975).

[*An impoverished room in a slummy, terraced house.*
VIVIAN *is drinking a mug of coffee, and watching* GARY *with growing consternation and alarm.*
GARY *is wearing a head-band with a feather sticking from it, dirty pullover and jeans. He's beginning to go into convulsions.*]

VIVIAN [*V.O.*]: My fifth husband was Gary. Home was now a twelve hundred pound dump that I bought with insurance money.

Gary was an orphan, a hardline junkie, an epileptic and a psychopath. But he really did love me: he threw hot coffee in my face, cut my eye open and smashed three of my ribs to prove it. But he always said he was sorry.

[GARY's *convulsions grow worse: he's dying.*
Sobbing hysterically, VIVIAN *holds him, trying to comfort him.*]

He died in front of my eyes from an overdose of drugs washed down with brandy. It was only *after* he died that it occurred to the doctor to mention he'd been having psychiatric treatment half his life. He had the mental age of an eight-year-old . . . and the medical profession didn't bother to tell me.

I loved Gary. But I think if he hadn't died, he'd have made damn sure *I* did. [*A pause.*] By hell . . . the jam butties I used to kiss in bed, as a kid. Wondering who'd I'd marry, would he be bonny, would he have a trade in his fingers . . . would he treat me right?

95. Ext. Gary's house. Day (1976).

[VIVIAN *comes out and gets into an old, dilapidated car.*]

VIVIAN [*V.O.*]: Today, 1976, my kids are at public school . . . paid for by the money Keith put in trust for them . . . and I'm on Social Security.

96. Ext. Kershaw Avenue. (Continuous in time).

[VIVIAN *is at the wheel of the car, driving slowly down the street.*]

VIVIAN [*V.O.*]: Not long ago, I went back to Kershaw Avenue, where we lived when we came up on the pools – just to see what it felt like . . . looked like. [*She stops the car.*]

97. Int. Car. Kershaw Avenue. (Continuous in time.)

[VIVIAN *sits looking calmly at the street. Silently, gently, she begins to cry.*]

VIVIAN [*V.O.*]: I looked. And I remembered everything. I thought if Motherwell had got another goal and Stockport not drawn with Oldham . . . we'd still be there.

Happen we'd have had the front room furnished by now. With its nice glass doors. To let the sunshine in.

They always say never look back. But sometimes it's the only way to *see* yourself. And it's then I understand why everything went wrong: because there was no *other* way it *could*'ve gone.

Maybe it's all my own fault. People like me aren't much good. You know, a bit sick. But there's *others* as bad. Happen a bit of it's *their* fault. Bank managers and newspapermen. The only difference is – *they* make a living out of it . . .

Money's a mystery to people like me – and Keith. We only understand a week's wages at a time. Happen that's all *some* folk *want* us to understand . . .

Newspapers, of course, are newspapers. The more you bugger up your life, the more they like it. [*Pause.*] Did you say you like a good laugh? Here's a good 'un for you . . . when we won the pools, we put a cross on the coupon for No Publicity.

I had some bad times in that street. *Bloody* bad. So bad I wanted to die. [*A beat.*] They were the best times I ever had.

THE END

FOR THE BEST IN PAPERBACKS, LOOK FOR THE

In every corner of the world, on every subject under the sun, Penguin represents quality and variety – the very best in publishing today.

For complete information about books available from Penguin – including Puffins, Penguin Classics and Arkana – and how to order them, write to us at the appropriate address below. Please note that for copyright reasons the selection of books varies from country to country.

In the United Kingdom: Please write to *Dept JC, Penguin Books Ltd, FREEPOST, West Drayton, Middlesex, UB7 0BR.*

If you have any difficulty in obtaining a title, please send your order with the correct money, plus ten per cent for postage and packaging, to *PO Box No 11, West Drayton, Middlesex*

In the United States: Please write to *Dept BA, Penguin, 299 Murray Hill Parkway, East Rutherford, New Jersey 07073*

In Canada: Please write to *Penguin Books Canada Ltd, 2801 John Street, Markham, Ontario L3R 1B4*

In Australia: Please write to the *Marketing Department, Penguin Books Australia Ltd, P.O. Box 257, Ringwood, Victoria 3134*

In New Zealand: Please write to the *Marketing Department, Penguin Books (NZ) Ltd, Private Bag, Takapuna, Auckland 9*

In India: Please write to *Penguin Overseas Ltd, 706 Eros Apartments, 56 Nehru Place, New Delhi, 110019*

In the Netherlands: Please write to *Penguin Books Netherlands B.V., Postbus 3507, NL–1001 AH, Amsterdam*

In West Germany: Please write to *Penguin Books Ltd, Friedrichstrasse 10–12, D–6000 Frankfurt/Main 1*

In Spain: Please write to *Alhambra Longman S.A., Fernandez de la Hoz 9, E–28010 Madrid*

In Italy: Please write to *Penguin Italia s.r.l., Via Como 4, I-20096 Pioltello (Milano)*

In France: Please write to *Penguin France S.A., 17 rue Lejeune, F-31000 Toulouse*

In Japan: Please write to *Longman Penguin Japan Co Ltd, Yamaguchi Building, 2–12–9 Kanda Jimbocho, Chiyoda-Ku, Tokyo 101*